Table of Contents

INTRODUCTION

CHAPTER ONE
ISSUES FACING THE USA

CHAPTER TWO
ISLAM'S TEACHINGS ACCORDING TO ISLAMIC SOURCES

CAN TRUMP DEFEAT HILLARY, OBAMA, ISLAMIC TERROR, PROSTITUTED MEDIA, AND POLITICAL PROSTITUTION

ABO-ELHAK EL-HAKANI

COPYRIGHT JUNE 2016

Edition 7, October 2016

(aboelhakelhakani@hotmail.com)

DEDICATION

TO ALL THE PEOPLE OF THE REAL DEMOCRATIC COUNTRIES THAT THE POLITICAL PROSTITUTES AND THE PROSTITUTED MEDIA STOLE THEIR FREEDOMS AND SOCIETIES.

TELL A PROSTITUTE WHY SHE IS, SHE WILL ACCUSE YOU OF ALL WHAT SHE DID.

(Tarek Farag)

****

TELL ME WHOM DO YOU SUPPORT, I TELL YOU WHO YOU ARE!

(Abo-Elhak El-Hakani)

****

Law enforcement personnel must apply the rule:

A SUSPECT IS POTENTIALLY GUILTY UNTIL PROVEN INNOCENT.

Courts apply the rule:

A DEFENDANT IS INNOCENT UNTIL PROVEN GUILTY.

(Tarek Farag)

****

In each case civilization is confronted with militant Mahommedanism. The forces of progress clash with those of reaction. The religion of blood and war is face to face with that of peace."

Winston S. Churchill

****

But that's always a certain way to recognize a fascist: when he's more powerful he kills everything that's different from him, he uses only brute force while law

2

breaks like glass under his boots. And then, when he loses and when he's weak, he invokes the law and tolerance of differences.

Andrej Nikolaidis
****

If Hillary Clinton were elected, she'd be the first president who couldn't pass a basic background check.

Donald Trump, Jr.
****

How many Americans have to die before Barak Obama and Hillary Clinton decide they can tell the truth about the threat to the United States from Islamic supremacists?

Newt Gingrich
****

Note:
The name <u>Hillastitutes</u> will be used to represent Ms. Hillary Clinton, Prostituted Media, and Political Prostitutes.

CHAPTER THREE
OBAMA'S ACTIONS AND INACTIONS

CHAPTER FOUR
COMMENTS ON THE NEWS

INTRODUCTION

Hillary, Obama, Obama's Administration, the Islamic Terror, the Political Prostitution, and the Prostituted Media, they are ganged together forming the political machine that controls the White House and the political life of the American people.

I noticed that Donald Trump was expressing his opinions as he sees them and **not acting like the political prostitutes that saturated our societies**. I analyzed his controversial political points of view and statements and found him to be correct almost all the times. His statement: "Crooked Hillary", shows that he is very nice, very polite, honest, and tells the truth. However, he needs to do many things differently. I feel that Trump is acting like a good soccer player playing against a very bad team. This bad team is trying to break his legs to win by illegal means. Instead of implementing his skills and cooperate with his team, he goes after his opponents to break their legs, and could end up having the referee kick him out of the game and **losing an easy win**. **Trump is distracted and dragged into side fighting and losing huge opportunities to obliterate his opponents, explain his positions, win his opponents to his side, and educate and inform the people inside and outside the USA**. One of these opportunities happened recently when a Pakistani lawyer attacked him about his positions towards Islam, which I will discuss as the first and most important issue in chapter 1.

Trump needs to understand that the Nation is putting all its hope on him to avoid the disastrous consequences if a **Career Criminal** is elected as the president of the USA. He needs to **lift himself above the dirty work** and let others do them instead. **Trump should win, and work for all** the USA's citizens including the supporters of his opponents, and he should appreciate his good luck that **Hillary is at least a proven careless liar**. Trump is used to run his business as the owner that takes the final decisions without any opposition, and gets all the responsibilities and credits for the successes and failures, while the US president should work with people that will oppose his final correct decisions just for opposition. To become the president, Trump needs to prove himself as a great leader. The **greatest leaders surround themselves with great leaders, to advice them** on different issues. The **worst leaders** surround themselves with **shameless liars**, and will fill the critical positions in their administration, especially the ones that **supposed to prosecute the corruption like the attorney general, with crooked and shameless corrupt people to share with them the plunder and protect each other**.

One of Trump's controversial positions is about Islam and Moslems. Since I already published the book "Islam's Teachings and Terror, The Full Truth, Islamophobia And The Political Prostitution", which is about the facts of Islam, I included it in this book as an academic reference, to explain the facts and the reasons behind Islamic Terror. In addition, I previously published the book: "Obama Vs. ISIS, Fiction Vs. Facts, Islamophobia And The Media, Forth World War", which discusses many of Obama's actions and statements, hence, I will add it also to save the time.

Although this presidential election looks as if mainly between Trump and Hillary, it is much more than this. **This election is simply a fierce fight by Obama, Hillary, and the full corruption machine to survive by making Hillary the president.** If Hillary becomes the president, she could destroy the USA for long period to come. **If Trump becomes the president, he could destroy this corruption machine and expose the largest fraud in the American history.**

I intended to write this book long time ago at the start of the rise of Donald Trump as a candidate for the presidency of the USA. However, I found myself running out of time, hence I had to publish this book quickly listing all the issues I see important to our country, and discusses in details the most important ones. Also, I added parts from my previous books as reference materials with minimum modifications. I hope that the readers will forgive me for my mistakes due to the time limits.

Since I found that, many people share the same opinions with me, and sometimes have better ideas; I am going to publish theirs here.

I love to hear from everyone his or her comments, either positive or negative, on the material in this book, by sending them to the email:

aboelhakelhakani@hotmail.com

CHAPTER ONE

ISSUES FACING THE USA

1. ISLAMIC TERROR

Trump's statements about Islamic terror and his suggestion to halt temporarily the coming of Moslems to the USA from Islamic countries, made many people misrepresent his statements to attack him. In reality, these **attacks exposed** the **misinformation** and the depth of the **political prostitution** in the USA and the world. Trump's statements were representing his own opinions supported by his own observations, not with deep study of the source of the Islamic terror or the actual teachings of Islam. However, if Trump knows the full truth about Islam, he could have strengthened his positions dramatically. Up until now, **Trump missed most of his golden opportunities to show the facts that support his positions, destroy his opponents, and expose to the entire world the sources of the Islamic terror**. One of these recent opportunities came to Trump on golden plate, when a Moslem Pakistani lawyer (Khizr Khan) that promotes the Islamic Sharia, attacked him for his position towards Islam. **Mr. Khan is representing millions of Moslems that share the same ideas**. Trump should have used it to start a good balanced civilized conversation in which both sides are present and not only the twisted peaceful Islam (as most of the media does), to clarify all the facts. **Trump should have used** this opportunity to **expose the true picture of Islam as practiced in reality** in Islamic countries, **not the way it is promoted outside the countries of Moslem majority** (or close to majority). Mr. Khan tried to **lecture Trump** and his supporters, and the country about the **US Constitution**, and ignored to tell us about **Pakistan's**

Constitution that: declares Islam as the State's religion, no law repugnant to Islam shall be enacted, and the Islamization of its present laws. Pakistan's constitution **erases all the human rights of all the non-Moslems and the Moslems that convert from Islam**. Even if we set aside Pakistan's inhumane and uncivilized constitution, and examine Mr. Khan's declaration of his affiliation with **Islam's teachings, which represent the most discriminative ideology. Islam's ideology goes far beyond discrimination** to the **criminalization of other** religions, ideologies, and different thinking of Islam itself (the entire world witnessed for centuries the brutal **Islamic killings** between Sunni and Shiite). This makes us wonder how he **dared to accuse Trump of promoting discrimination against Islam or Moslems**. All what Trump asked for was to halt the coming of Moslems to the USA until we can figure out a way to allow them to come without threatening our citizens. Mr. Trump did not ask for the **USA to treat Moslems as Islamic countries treat non-Moslems**. Mr. Trump did not call for the **killings** of Moslems, **expulsions** of Moslems, **lootings** of Moslem's properties, **destruction** of Mosques, denying permits to build or repair Mosques, **kidnapping** of Moslems' **underage girls** to convert them to other religions, or any of the actions in a **long list** of **atrocities that are the normal life for Christians in Islamic countries**. To demonstrate it clearly, let me take Egypt as another Islamic country, which Obama considers it a moderate Islamic country that has a **president that calls for the illusion of the reform of Islam** (knowing that any change in its teachings, or different interpretations of them is a **blasphemy punishable by death**). In Egypt, **building a church or the gathering of Christians to pray, is considered a sever offense to Moslems and a threat to the national security**. A permit to **repair or build a church** is so **outrageously dangerous** that requires the **approval of all security agencies** on all levels, requires a minimum processing period of **10 years**, and finally requires the **approval of Egypt's president**. Even after going through the processes, and getting the long waited permit, every thing could be canceled for no reason (an example of this a church is closed now for 30 years after its completion). [https://www.gatestoneinstitute.org/7433/egypt-churches], [http://www.state.gov/j/drl/rls/irf/2005/51598.htm]. I expect that Mr. Khan will **respond** using the **deceptive statements** used by Obama and others, that these **atrocities do not belong to**

Islam. I am discussing the deceptions of these statements in Chapter 2 "Teachings Of Islam By Islamic Sources". Additionally, there is **no right for non-USA citizens to come** to the USA. It is the opposite, there are **regulations to prevent the people that could threaten us or do not respect our constitution** from coming to the USA. Mr. Khan fell into a **fatal mistake** when he lectured us that the US Constitution would not discriminate against the religion of Islam. He ignored to lecture us about the fact that **Islam is against all the basic human freedoms**. He did not realize that the **US Constitution does not recognize Islam as a religion, and guarantees only the NON-VIOLENT practices of the freedoms of religions, expression, and speech**. The definition of religion is "The belief in and worship of a superhuman controlling power, especially a personal God or gods", which does not apply to Islam because Moslems consider Islam a full system to all aspects of life including religion. While the definition of an ideology is "A **system of ideas** and ideals that are the basis of economical, political, criminal, and civil laws", which matches the teachings of Islam. This shows that **Islam is an Ideology, which does not even qualify** to the protection of a religion under the USA's constitution. The Islamic ideology **does not even qualify** for the **protection of speech or expression** because of its **violent teachings, and the constitution guarantees only the peaceful practices of these freedoms** . Even if we assume that Islam could be categorized as a religion, the USA's constitution **does not give protection to religions** just because they are religions. **In fact, the constitution stands firmly against any practices that violate our laws**. The best example for this is that many of the Mormons' practices are forbidden and punishable by the law. Let me make it clear again, that **the USA's Constitution never supported the call for violence or any violent practices of religions, speech, or expression**. Similarly, Mr. Khan knows well that the practicing of **many Islamic rules**, that are **lawful under Sharia**, are not only incompatible with our system, but also violates our laws and could be considered **sever criminal offenses**. Hence, people saying that Islam is incompatible with our system, need to say it more accurately that **Islam's teachings contradict our system**. If Mr. Khan was caring about this country, he should have **called for Moslems that believe in Sharia law and crying discrimination, to respect our constitution and system and move to** other countries that have laws compatible with Sharia. However, he needs to remind them that the **US laws protect "Animal Rights" better than the "Human Rights" in many of those Islamic countries**. Since I mentioned "Animal Rights", I need to draw the attention to the practices of **animal-sacrifice** mandated on Moslems on one of the biggest feasts in Islam "Eid Eladha", which violates animal's rights. If Mr. Khan was caring about Islam, he **should have lectured Moslems** and Islamic countries **to respect the basic human rights.** instead of **lecturing a civilized country that hosted him and gave him this opportunity to give his deceptive hateful speech**. In reality, **Islam is qualified for a special act, similar to the Ku Klux Klan Act of 1871**, which was acted to protect the black citizens from the Klan's terror. **Strangely enough**, Mr. Khan surpassed Mr. Trump in proving to us that the **citizens of the USA need urgently a special act to protect them, SPECIFICALLY, from the Islamic intimidations and terror in all their forms**. We need to realize that **Islamic terror is not limited to physical terror of killings and torture; it includes MENTAL TERROR, CULTURAL TERROR**, etc.

Additionally, when someone apply to **migrate to the USA, he is** asked if he **agrees with polygamy or communism**, an answer yes to any one, was enough to **prevent him from coming to the USA. Why it is inappropriate for Trump** to suggest something to protect our lives and prevent **repeating brutal killings**, while **marrying more than one wife** is not going to kill anyone?!

Now, let me inform Mr. Trump and the World, and remind Mr. Khan, Obama, and other Moslems, about the following **Islamic facts**, for which I need to know their **honest opinions** about how they judge these facts, and how they would relate them to the actions of Islamic Terrorists:

1. The prophet Mohammad, by himself, in one day, and with his sword, **cutoff the heads** of all men in the **Jewish tribe** of Bani Koriza (estimated between 600 to 1000), **for no valid reason**. He took all their women and children as slaves, and took their lands, properties, and money for himself and his army.

2. The prophet Mohammad, by himself **cutoff the 2 hands, and the 2 feet, and gauged the 2 eyes** of eight men because they converted from Islam.

3. All the Jewish tribe of Bani-El-Nadier (about 500 families, except two men) refused to accept Mohammad as a prophet

and preferred to be expelled out from their lands and their ancestors' lands instead of converting to Islam.

4. The prophet Mohammad ordered the **assassinations** of many people including **women** for criticizing him or Islam. Some of them were: a) Om Kerfa: A high ranking old woman that was killed by splitting her by tying her legs to 2 camels moving in opposite directions. b) Asmaa Bent-Marawan: Wrote a poem criticizing Moslems for killing people, and she was killed by stabbing a sword into her chest coming out of her back when she was asleep. c) Kaab Ebn-Alashraf: A high ranking man criticized Mohammad. Mohammad's people lured and deceived him, and cut off his head.

5. The prophet Mohammad sent his army to catch a precious caravan loaded with gold and silver that tried to pass away from him. The men of the caravan were terrified and escaped leaving everything without any resistance. The Islamic sources consider it a jihad battle, and called it the battle of Alkerdah.

6. **Quran orders Moslems to cut off the heads of the disbelievers**; "When you meet the faithless, strike their necks. When you have thoroughly decimated them, bind the captives firmly. Thereafter either release them or take ransom until the war lays down its burdens. That (is Allah's ordinance), and had Allah wished He could have taken vengeance on them, but that He may test some of you by means of others. As for those who were slain in the way of Allah, He will not let their works go awry." [47:4].

7. Here are some statements of the **Quran ordering the killings of non-Moslems** (disbelievers): "O you who believe! Kill those of the disbelievers who are near you, and let them find harshness in you, and know that Allah is with those who keep their duty (unto Him)." [9:123]. "Kill in the way of Allah, and know that Allah is Hearer, Knower." [2:244]. "Mohammad is the messenger of Allah. And those with him are harsh against the disbelievers and merciful among themselves." [48:29].

8. **Quran makes Islam the only religion** acceptable to Allah "And whoever desires a religion other than Islam, it shall not be accepted from him, and in the hereafter he shall be one of the losers."[3:85].

9. There are huge numbers of Quran's statements ordering Moslems to kill non-Moslems; some of them are stated in other parts of this book.

2. TERROR IS WINNING THE WAR WHILE WE ARE FAILING TO PROTECT OURSELVES

In wars, the winner is the one who imposes his will on the other. It is clear that the terrorists imposed their will on us; they are frightening us everywhere, causing huge losses of lives (military and civilians), many injuries, and huge losses of properties, costing us tremendous amounts of money and trillions of dollars for the military. For people to estimate, just the cost of terror to our air transportation industry, we have about 800 million passengers a year (2015 Airline Traffic Data, http://www.rita.dot.gov/bts/press_releases/bts015_16), the direct airport security fees is $5.6, the average lost time per passenger is about 1.5 hour, for average hourly rate of $25/hr, will result in money losses of about **$34,480,000,000** per year. **SPENDING FEW MILLIONS OF DOLLARS PER YEAR TO ESTABLISH SATELLITE TV STATIONS - NOT MILITARY SATELLITES - TO EDUCATE THE PEOPLE AROUND THE WORLD WITH DIFFERENT LANGUAGES, ABOUT THE REAL TEACHINGS OF ISLAM AND THE REAL HUMAN RIGHTS, WILL CERTAINLY FIGHT THIS TERROR MUCH BETTER, WITH A COST LESS THAN THAT OF A SINGLE FIGHTER JET.**
In spite of all the tremendous money we spent, up until now, we are unable to stop the terrorists. **Our country's Security Agencies proved to us their complete failure, even when they are informed early enough about terrorists**. However, **OBAMA AND OTHER HEADS OF OUR NATIONAL SECURITY AGENCIES, DO NOT FEEL THAT THEY ARE RESPONSIBLE, AND NONE OF THEM**

RESIGNED, CHANGED HIS/HER FAILED POLICIES, OR WAS FIRED.

The people that are responsible about protecting us, **lost their goals, and made their original tools their goals and their goals became their tools**. To explain this; originally the goals of those agencies were to protect us and keep us safe. Their tools to protect us, was to get powers to monitor and spy on people, get certain exceptional powers to arrest and search people, - - etc. However, they are using the fight against terror (original goal) as a tool (excuse) to achieve their new twisted goals of getting more powers to spy on people, arrest and search people, - - etc. **Their goals became to get more powers to spy on people, and used the war on terror as an excuse to get these powers** (fighting terror is not their goal anymore).

The **FBI** and other security agencies, **failed miserably without any excuse** to protect us from the disastrous actions of Islamic terror. One example was demonstrated in the San Bernardino massacre, and the FBI's fight with Apple that followed. Additionally, the disastrous failure to prevent **Florida's Nightclub massacre**. The FBI's main job is to **prevent** things from happening, not to ignore the leads, and not to wait after the disaster, and find who did it. What is the value of arresting or killing someone after he kills and injures tens of innocent people? The FBI had the power, the laws, and the opportunity to listen and record all the terrorists' communications, but they **did not do it**, and later try to hide their **failures and blame them on Apple**. **The amazing thing is that no one resigned, or was held accountable.**

3. I MUST GET ALL NOBEL PRIZES FOR DISCOVERING THE CONNECTION BETWEEN THE ACTS OF TERRORISTS

Commenting on the knife attack in Minnesota and the bombs in NJ, on Sep. 19, 2016, Obama, the <u>COMMANDER IN CHEAT</u> said;

"Meanwhile, while all this is going on in New York and New Jersey, we're also focused on the stabbing attack at the shopping mall in Minnesota. **At this point, we see no connection between that incident and what happened here in New York and New Jersey**."
[https://www.bostonglobe.com/news/nation/2016/09/19/read-obama-statement-nyc-blasts/GajTTnaleTEfvnC3fl6kzJ/story.html]

To find out the connection that Obama could not find in this attack and other terrorist actions, I examined the following facts:
- San Bernardino terrorist Syed Rizwan Farook is Moslem;
- San Bernardino terrorist Tashfeen Malik is Moslem;
- Orlando nightclub terrorist Omar Mateen is Moslem;
- Obama that occupies the position of the president is Moslem;
- Hillary's top aid Huma Abdin is Moslem;
- Jeh Johnson Homeland Security Secretary is pro-Moslems;
- Fatima Noor Asst. Dir. US Citizenship and Immigration (Policy Analyst for Immigration and Rural Affairs) is Moslem;
    - - - - - - - -
- **Trump** wants to limit and examine the coming of Moslems.

Now after all the previous facts, as an idiot, I concluded with **100%** certainty that the **connection between that incident and what happened here in New York and New Jersey** is **Trump**. I think because **I am so smart and concluded something that no other idiot can come to, I must receive all the Nobel Prizes in all fields.**

4. THE POLITICAL PROSTITUTION

Prostitution is known as the engagement in sexual relations in exchange for money or some other benefit. People were engaged in prostitution to exchange benefits; the prostitute will gain financial benefits, and her customer will gain sexual pleasure. In some places, prostitution is legal. Similarly, in politics, we can see **politicians engaged in exchanges of benefits with their client,** whom I call "**Political Prostitutes**". In sexual prostitution, the prostitute is selling **only her own body**, but in Political Prostitution, the **politician is selling his country, his society, his position, the future of his people, and himself.** Also, the client is forced to **pay to get benefits and/or avoid harm. Political prostitute is similar to a wife cheating on her husband and giving his property to her clients**. Unfortunately, the USA is **saturated with political prostitutes** in every field. Some of them are **illegal prostitutes** and others are **amazingly legal prostitutes**, the most precarious of whom are the political representatives and the judges. The dangers of the political prostitutes increase in proportion to their ranks, and reach their climax when a **prostitute holds international position or deals with foreign rich countries**. Additionally, our political system is filled with **illegal** and **legal thieves**. A disaster will happen when a **political prostitute is also a thieve**.

I was amazed when watching the preparation for the presidential elections for 2016, and seeing how the political prostitutes competed openly with each other, to offer cheaper prices for their clients, while ignoring completely the wellbeing, interests, and safety of the American people. Moreover, I was amazed to see those prostitutes brag about the down payments they received; and the money they legally and illegally collected, and **falsely claim that these payments will have no effect on their future decisions** (what an honest prostitutes and thieves).

The easiest way to know how many political prostitutes we have, is to watch our congress when they examine someone that did something wrong like Hillary Clinton.

5. THE PROSTITUTED MEDIA

Unfortunately, we have a large number of prostituted media, which try to deceive and misguide the American people. As I said before, a regular prostitute sells her body only, while a political prostitute or a prostituted media sell their country, the country's future, and anything they can reach. Those prostituted media hide the facts and twist them in every possible way to favor the people that bought them. One simple example, when the **massacre of Florida's club happened**, all the **prostituted media were extremely concerned that it could prove that Trump is truthful, and Islam's teachings is the cause of the Islamic terror**, while showing little concern for the **safety of the American** people.

The teachings of Islam were known and applied for more than thousand years. However, the devastating effect of Jihad on the civilized world, started to show recently due to the technological improvements of exchanging and transferring the information. Part of this technology at the beginning was the media, which was mainly the television and broadcasting, and later the internet. Unfortunately, **most of the media conspired to deceive the world about the realty of Jihad**, for political and/or financial reasons. They were biased while pretending to be neutral. One good example is the movie that a US citizen made and caused barbaric reactions from Moslems all over the world. **Instead of harshly criticizing those barbaric actions, they attacked and blamed this US citizen for practicing his human rights, without giving him the opportunity to defend himself or even explain his point of view**. Further, the media went into a **deception** campaigns to give the impression that Islam is a **peaceful and tolerant religion**. They allowed only the opinions of members of Islamic organizations like **CAIR** (affiliated with Muslim Brotherhood), and hide the opinions of other people that studied Islam and Jihad well. On the other hand, they distracted the attention of people to other non-important issues like the problems in the Catholic Church (not the grave violations of human rights in Islamic countries).

6. OBAMA'S DIVISIVE WAR BETWEEN BLACKS AND WHITE OFFICERS

I am one of the people that voted for Obama for the first term knowing that he is a Moslem and black. It was one of my happiest days when he became president. This proved to me, that the **US is**

the greatest nation on earth. Not because of its military might, economical power, or technological advancements, but **because of its civilized citizens and laws**. Nowhere in the world a similar thing ever happened, or can happen. I thought that **being freely elected** to be the president of the greatest nation would make him call on all the minorities to realize that all the limits to their dreams were destroyed. Sadly, I was devastated, like many others, when I found out that his actions were **anti-American, anti-Constitution, and pro-Islam**. His actions revealed to me that **his election was a fraud played by him, petro-dollars, and other evil powers**.

Mr. Barack Hussein Obama, US Attorney General, Hillary Clinton, and others, started a war between blacks and the law enforcement officers, especially white officers. **They want to set the country on fire to claim that Trump caused it, and then Hillary will come, unite, and save the nation!!?** They intentionally misrepresented the facts many times, to give the impression that the law enforcement officers in the whole country are unfairly targeting Blacks and Hispanics, which resulted in the despicable immediate assassination of four police officers in Texas, the death of other officers, and will result in more deaths in the future. We can see the expansion of the unacceptable violence and riots of Blacks spreading to different states.

Few hours after Mr. Barack Hussein Obama, stated his misleading facts, 4 police officers were assassinated.
http://www.gopusa.com/obama-lectures-nation-on-racial-disparities-hours-before-assassination-of-dallas-police-officers/
He induced the perpetrators to be violent against the law enforcement personnel (especially Whites) by saying the following:

1. African Americans are **30% more** likely than whites to be pulled over. After being pulled over, African Americans and Hispanics are **3 times** more likely to be searched.
2. African Americans were **shot by police** at more than **twice the rate of whites**.
3. African Americans are **arrested at twice** the rate of whites.
4. African American defendants are **75% more likely** to be charged with offenses carrying mandatory minimums.
5. They receive sentences that are almost **10% longer** than comparable whites arrested for the same crime.

21

6. The **African American and Hispanic** population (**30%** of the general population) makes up more than **50%** of the incarcerated population.
7. **Blacks and Hispanics** feel that they are discriminated against, and they are hurt.
8. All Americans should be very angry for that discrimination.

When examining the statistics on Race and **Violent Crime (VC)**, prepared by Obama's DOJ [http://www.amren.com/news/2015/07/new-doj-statistics-on-race-and-violent-crime/], it will show that during the 2012/2013 period:

A) Blacks committed an average of 560,600 VC against Whites, whereas Whites committed only 99,403 VC against Blacks. This means **Blacks were the attackers in 84.9% (5.62 times Whites' attacks)**.

B) **Blacks are the attackers 82.5% against Hispanics (4.71** times Hispanic's attacks).

C) From the figures for the 2013 racial mix of the population - 62.2% white, 17.1% Hispanic, 13.2% black - a **black is 27 times more likely to attack a white and 8 times more likely to attack a Hispanic. A Hispanic is 8 times more likely to attack a white**.

D) The rate of **VC per person** (relative to whites) is **2.46 for Blacks, 1.255 for Hispanics**.

E) The statistic show that Whites VC against Blacks is **3.6%**, when normalized to **62.2%** (white population percentage) will give **5.788%** (0.036/0.622 = 0.0578778). And Blacks VC against Whites is **38.6%**, when normalized to 13.2% will give **292.4%** (0.386/0.132 = 2.924). **The ratio of the number of Blacks' normalized Violent Crimes against Whites, to the number of Whites' normalized Violent Crimes against Blacks is staggering 5052%.**

According to these statistics, **Obama, the COMMANDER IN CHEAT, is <u>misleading</u> the Nation to believe that <u>Blacks and Hispanics are discriminated against, while the truth is the opposite, as follow</u>:**

1- African Americans are **<u>30% more</u>** likely than whites to be pulled over, while they should be **<u>246% to 562% more</u>** likely (see D and **A** above). After being pulled over, African Americans and Hispanics are **<u>3 times</u>** more likely to be searched, while searching Blacks should be **<u>2.46 to 27 times</u>** and Hispanics **<u>1.26 to 8 times</u>** (see C and D above).

2- African Americans were **<u>shot by police</u>** at more than **twice** the rate of whites, while this shooting should be **<u>2.46 to 27 times</u>** (see C and D above).

3- African Americans are **<u>arrested at twice</u>** the rate of whites, while it should be **<u>2.46 to 27 that rate</u>** (see C and D).

4- African American defendants are **<u>75% more likely</u>** to be charged with offenses carrying mandatory minimums, while it should be **<u>245% to 562% more likely</u>** (see A, D).

5- They receive sentences that are almost **<u>10% longer</u>** than comparable whites arrested for the same crime, while it should be **<u>245% to 562% longer</u>** (see A, D).

6- **Blacks and Hispanics** feel that they are **<u>discriminated against, and they are HURT</u>**. This statement is **<u>irresponsible, and deceptive</u>**, because the calculations done here show that police is actually favoring Blacks and Hispanics. It is an open invitation to **<u>violence</u>** against White police officers to stop hurting Blacks and Hispanics.

7- **<u>All Americans should be very angry for the untruthful discrimination presented by Obama.</u>**

<u>All Americans must demand the prosecution of Obama, and any and all other persons, that commit the same actions that can threaten our law enforcement personnel or the peace in our societies, as any citizen committing the same acts. We demand them to stop threatening our law enforcement officers, and to let our police officers do their jobs fairly without favoring Blacks and/or Hispanics</u>.

Obama and his gang, instead of crying for; the innocent black people that Blacks kill daily, and the large disproportionate number of Blacks' VC against Whites and Hispanics, they are trying to deceive the country and **start a race war to accuse Trump of initiating it**.

We must acknowledge that the **police responded the wrong way in some incidents, but they were not targeting anyone**. They were following certain procedures, some of which must be changed. We should not ignore the difficult situations facing the law enforcement personnel when they try to do their jobs and **protect the lives and properties** of people, especially when they deal with **people known for their high potential of violence**. They **must apply the following rule, especially for Islamic terrorists**:

A SUSPECT IS POTENTIALLY GUILTY UNTIL PROVEN INNOCENT.

While in **courts**:

A DEFENDANT IS INNOCENT UNTIL PROVEN GUILTY.

7. ILLEGAL IMMIGRANTS

I am amazed for the people, and the political prostitutes, that ignore the meaning of the English word "**ILLEGAL**" in the English sentence "**ILLEGAL immigrants**". Illegal simply means contrary to or forbidden by law. **Any country that does not enforce its laws, and allow anyone, its citizens, foreigners, or others to disrespect or to violate its laws, are DOOMED FOR DESTRUCTION**. We are a democratic country, where our

Congress enacts our laws. If any of our laws is too old to apply, or becomes unfair, or people feel the need to change it, **our Congress and only our Congress**, should change it. It is **unconstitutional and illegal** for the **president** to change any law or its application **by any kind of executive order**. However, we have a corrupt president that was teaching the law, and swore to **preserve, protect and defend the Constitution of the United States**, but does not care or respect our constitution or our laws, and issue illegal orders. We must vehemently reject giving any kind of legal status to illegal immigrants other than that specified in our laws.

Because we have large number of illegal immigrants, the waiting period for legal immigrants became excessively long and unfair. This large number of illegal immigrants delayed the legal immigration of legal immigrants by a time that could be 15 years or more. After which, family members of the legal ones could be disqualified from immigrating with them, because they will pass the age limit (for example a 7 years old child will be 22 passing the age of 18 and 21), **causing the separation of the families or preventing the entire family from migrating**. Those who **cry for the separation of the families of the ILLEGAL immigrants**, how could they **justify the separation of the families of the legal migrants.** Additionally, for a legal immigrants at the ages of 40 or 45, to migrate after a delay of 15 years, they **will come** to the USA at ages of 55 to 60, at which they are **about to retire and start losing their energy**. This makes it extremely difficult for them to start a new life or effectively add to the economy. This could make them a burden on the society not an addition.

Some people claim that illegal immigrants are needed for our economy because they accept working under harsh conditions that Americans will not accept them. This is a bad argument, and those people, are the **ones that call for human treatment to the illegal immigrants, however, they twist the facts and try to keep them to work under inhumane conditions** we do not allow them for animals. Others argue that illegal immigrants provide **cheap labor to farmers** and keep the prices of local farm products low, I disagree. First, the percentage of illegal immigrants working in farming is small. Second, if this percentage is high, this argument could be true for the short run, but **for the long run, it is very harmful**. The **advancements** in the technologies, especially machine vision, made many **automated and robotic machines** able to do the work of thousands of those humans, under **extremely harsh conditions**, for a fraction of the cost and at speeds and efficiencies much higher than humans. I found hundreds of patents in this field; very few of them are implemented, because the initial investments to execute those patents are difficult to justify against the competition of cheap human labor. However, once the cheap labor is removed, those machines will come to the market at high prices at the beginning, but will get much cheaper and better very quickly. The impact of developing those machines will go beyond the USA, or the farming. We will be able to **export those machines to other countries and add a large number of high-technology jobs to our labor market, and a huge income to our economy**. Those machines will allow us to compete in farming products even at the least expensive labor markets.

Some people, some political prostitutes, and the prostituted media, try to twist the facts and the statements of Trump and **implicate him** in bad things against Hispanics. In reality, **illegal immigrants are harming the Hispanics communities the most**, because of the same reasons, I just discussed. Trump did not single out Hispanics; he is talking about all illegal immigrants. It happened that the main sources of illegal immigrants are coming through our **borders with Mexico, and we must stop them. Building a wall**, reforming the immigration laws, or **any other action** should be determined after his election. I am certain that Trump will change the way he will handle the illegal immigration, as he indicated that he would keep the dignity of the people. It is like an **honest judge trying to apply the law to a poor man that stole food for few dollars; he must keep the law and use the available options to be fair**. At least, **TRUMP IS THE ONLY ONE TALKING FAIRLY, LEGALLY, AND HONESTLY ABOUT THE ISSUE OF ILLEGAL IMMIGRANTS WITHOUT FEAR FROM LOSING THE VOTES OF HISPANICS**.

Some people are proposing a good solution to this illegal immigrants' issue. It includes **shortening the waiting period for legal** migrants and **bringing them quickly** to the USA to replace the illegal ones. This will open the doors for **illegals to leave** by themselves knowing that their turn to **come back legally** will be reasonably short. Imposing **large fines** on people that **hire illegals** and the illegals themselves, enough to **cover the cost of**

deportation many times. After certain period of time, anyone illegally present in the USA, will lose forever his ability to migrate, and will be fined and deported and the person that was sheltering him will be fined also.

8. THE HIDDEN BUSINESS OF OBAMA AND HILLARY WITH TERRORISTS
(This part is intentionally repeated)

The son of Khairat al-Shatter (top ranking Brotherhood member), threatened to expose documents that would land Obama in prison. In addition, Morsi's wife threatened to publish letters from Hillary Clinton, exposing her **business relationship with Hillary**, **"special relationship" between Muslim Brotherhood and Obama's Administration, and the support Obama got from the Muslim Brotherhood for his election and reelection**
[http://www.albawabhnews.com/293820],
[http://www.jihadwatch.org/2014/08/morsis-wife-threatens-to-publish-letters-from-hillary-clinton-exposing-special-relationship-between-muslim-brotherhood-and-obama-administration].
Egyptian Official Tahani al-Gebali (Vice President of the Supreme Constitutional Court in Egypt) claimed to have proof and documents that could send Obama to prison. These documents would explain why the Obama administration is so vehemently supportive of the Muslim Brotherhood, whose terrorism, has among other atrocities, caused the destruction of some 80 Christian churches in less than one week
[http://freedomoutpost.com/2013/08/second-source-egyptian-official-tahanial-gebali-claims-to-have-documents-proof-that-could-send-obama-to-prison/].
The **Egyptian government** has a wealth of **documents** about the **support of Hillary and Obama to the Moslem Brotherhood and terrorists**. They did not disclose them; they could be using them as **extortion** tool.

9. IRAN

Iran is one of the best examples for Islamic destruction, Islamic terror, and the complete failure of the USA. Iran was a civilized country with rich history. Iran's people are not Arabs, and feel offended when some one tries to relate them to Arabs; they consider Arabs invaders that destroyed their culture. Iranians were hoping to modernize their country after they nationalized their oil industry in 1951, but the British and the **American** orchestrated a coup that put back in power the Shah in 1953. The Iranians succeeded in doing some reforms and modernizations during the Shah's ruling. However, the Shah (was fully supported by the USA) adopted **autocratic policies that made people revolt** against him. The Islamists (Ayatollah) lead the revolution, which in reality was that they stole the Iranian revolution. The **Iranian people did not revolt because they could not practice freely their religion, they revolted against things that has nothing to do with religion**. After Ayatollahs came to power and declaring Iran an **Islamic country and applying Sharia laws, everything deteriorated** and large number of highly educated men and women fled Iran. The world started seeing a full display of the **destruction of the society and the violations of the human rights in Iran after applying the Islamic laws**, which is a **lesson for every one that ignores the Islamic threats**.

Obama's friendship with Iran is coming from his pro-Islam ideology, to bring into the international community a different Islamic country (Shiite Islam). Although **Obama's intentions are evil**, they will lead to the enforcement of the secular ideologies in Iran, which **could reduce the impact of the Islamists and reform** the country.

Israel is the best country that can make the best Iranian nuclear deal, which should be applied equally to all countries including Israel itself.

10.   HEALTHCARE

Trump's proposal to open the market for healthcare insurance companies from out of states, cannot reduce the cost or improve the services as he wishes. Trump knows from his business experience that increasing the number of brokers competing in a limited market will eventually **reduce the brokerage cost, but increase the price**. Trump knows that the only way to control the prices is through the **equation of demand and supply**.

The author Tarek Farag published the book "Trump The Only One That Can Adopt This Best Healthcare Plan", which I agree with most of his points. Farag's plan starts by setting the goals and features and moved to achieve them in a simple logical way. I am going to summarize his "Healthcare Plan" here, and the reader can refer to the book for further details.

Features of proposed healthcare plan:

Healthcare is a human right in which all citizens should have the same minimum coverage irrespective of the wealth of the individuals. Poor and low-income people are the ones that need it most at low cost, because rich people can afford better coverage.

Healthcare is the responsibility of the government towards all citizens, which removes the burdens from employers; and encourage the employees to develop their career without fear for their health.

Healthcare should be delivered quickly and effectively, without risky delays.

Healthcare's expenses are not luxury expenses, and should be tax deductible without limitations.

All citizens must pay the same percentage of their income (Healthcare Tax) to finance the system irrespective of their income or health condition.

The strategy to control the cost should be to implement the natural law of supply and demand, not by applying artificial forces like mandating healthcare providers to provide services below their cost. We should reduce the demand by preventive healthcare [immunization, healthy lifestyle, regular exams, etc.], and implement the forces that promote the increase of supply.

Healthcare Companies:

The measure of success in healthcare companies is the profits they make, not the services they provide. The role of healthcare companies is that of unnecessary brokers. They collect money from participants, pay health care providers, pay their costs, and keep their profits. Their method of reducing the cost is to reduce the services, which is harmful to the participants, or reduce the payments to healthcare providers, which could be harmful to the providers. Hence, the best way to provide health care at minimum cost is to eliminate or reduce the profits of healthcare companies, which will drive them out of business eliminating them, and their employees could be trained as healthcare providers.

We conclude that, a governmental organization is the best one to manage healthcare. Fortunately, we have the federal program MEDICARE that we can modify, improve, and finance. When we give all the money that the healthcare companies collect and put them in MEDICARE, we will be able to provide services at better level to the current participants. However, we must add taxes to finance the services for the currently uncovered people (most of them of low income).

Healthcare Personnel:

The healthcare personnel are doctors, nurses, specialists, technicians, etc. Currently, we have shortage in the supplies of these professionals and unable to meet the demands for their services. The natural result of the demand exceeding the supply is an increase in the price, and depriving needy people from the services. This shortage of personnel is reflected in different forms affecting the level of the healthcare services and its availability. For example, rich people that can afford good healthcare could schedule an operation or an expensive MRI within few days, while others have to wait couple of months to schedule the same operation or go through additional approval steps delaying the MRI, which is unfair and inhumane. When implementing an AFFORDABLE (almost free) healthcare system, we should expect a huge increase in the demand, which will exceed the already low existing capacity. We must increase the supplies of healthcare personnel immediately, irrespective of applying this proposed system or not.

Increasing the number of healthcare personnel could be done very easily by increasing the number of healthcare students;

providing them with education loans; and improving their study and training systems. To attract qualified students to become healthcare professionals, we need to compensate them fairly when they practice their profession according to their responsibilities, length and cost of study, etc.

Healthcare Facilities:
We need to increase the number of healthcare facilities to decrease the cost, which can happen as a natural result for increasing the supply of healthcare professionals that will need an increased space for their practice.

Prescription Drugs and Medical Equipment and their Research:
The research, development, and manufacturing of prescription drugs and medical equipment are strategic industries that we must keep at the top, and preserve them inside the USA and not to let them migrate to outside. Importing drugs from foreign countries, especially the ones without regulations comparable to that of the USA, is extremely dangerous.

Again, the measure of success for pharmaceutical companies is the profit. Selling products at the maximum price (some call it "greed"), is the normal and acceptable goal of successful companies. **Pharmaceutical companies must have an ETHICAL CODE OF CONDUCT at high standard**. It is difficult and counterproductive for the government to interfere to set the price or the profit margins for drugs. **We see outrageous greed from some pharmaceutical** companies that **exploded the prices** of certain drugs that they monopolize for **no reason other than greed**. Currently the US **government is funding many research** activities for new drugs, but after their success, they let **large pharmaceutical** companies buy their rights, which is wrong. In these cases, it is better to let the companies bid on marketing of these drugs to the lowest bidder for royalty not a lump sum payment. To reduce the prices of drugs we need to reduce the manufacturing cost when possible, and increase the supply to meet or exceed the demand, without sacrificing the quality.

When talking about FDA approved prescription drugs, we can divide them into two kinds:

(1) Drugs not protected by patents (easy to control their price increase).

(2)   Drugs with unexpired patents.

The best way to discover new drugs and equipment and sell them at reasonable prices is to establish research centers run by the government, government with universities, or universities. The basic salaries of the researchers in these centers should be lower than the salaries of comparable researchers in pharmaceutical companies. However, they should be paid royalties to attract the best researchers.

The most important matter in drug development is the IP (Intellectual Property), which could be protected by trade secrets or patents. **The current patenting system is unfit and unfair, especially for drugs**, which will be discussed later.

Healthcare Liabilities:

The compensations for victims of doctor's errors are usually extremely unfair and could be tens of millions of dollars, while the victims of murder are rarely compensated beyond a million. Tens of inventions are not implemented because of the liability cost and the approval processes. We must implement tort reform.

Patient's Co-pay:

To avoid the abuse associated with free or almost free services, we need to have the patient pay reasonable co-pay. In case that the person is unable to pay it, the system should pay it for them in the form of **loans into the system** (nothing free), to be paid later on installments, or when they can get enough income. This is a better replacement to health savings or accounts (like Flex Plan).

Patent System Reform

The current patenting system is unfair to inventors, especially the small ones. It encourages big companies to steal the small inventors, or wait until the patentees cannot afford to keep paying the patent fees and lose their patents. Also, small inventors cannot protect their inventions in other countries, which allow big companies to use their patents in those foreign countries without any compensation. Additionally, a small inventor in the medical field cannot afford the expenses of approving his invention.

Trump was the only one to discuss or mention the protection of the Intellectual property. This demonstrated that **Trump is the only**

one that understands the huge importance of the IPs in general, and in particular its huge impact on the healthcare technology. economy and the development of our technology. We need to change the patent laws to protect the small inventor, and encourage the research and development.

We would like to see the extension of the protection period for a patent, and the elimination or reduction of all the fees related to patents for small and micro entities. And most importantly, is the **expansion of the protection of the patents issued in the USA, to be protected in the entire world** without applying for it repeatedly in all the countries. Governments can collect **patent-protection-fees in the form of a small percentage of the sale price** of each product sold under patent protection, which could be much higher than the different patent fees of application, examination, maintenance, etc. For example, assume that we have a tool that was selling for $10.00, at a volume of 10,000 per year, and someone improved it under a patent, and was able to sell it under this patent protection for $11.00, at the same volume of 10,000, then charging a patent-protection-fee of 0.5% of the sale price (5.5 cents), will generate $550.00 per year as revenues for the patent office, which could be higher than the patent fees. However, the volume of an improved product runs in the millions, which could generate revenues for this inexpensive product in the range of tens of thousands of dollars per year, which is much better for the government and the inventor. Additionally, if a product is protected under three patents, then the patent-protection-fee will be tripled. Needless to say that, most of the drugs protected by patents have sales volumes **above billions** of dollars, which generates for this single drug, **patent-protection-fees exceeding couple millions** of dollars. This proposed patent system will charge small fees for small inventions and proportionally large fees for large inventions.

11.   THE CORRUPT LEGAL SYSTEM

We all know that without a JUST justice system, corruption and crimes will spread destroying our civilized society (if we have one).

In reality, we have a **corrupt justice system of all kinds at all levels, STARTING FROM THE SUPREME COURT down to every aspects of our justice system**. People expressed the corruption of the legal system in funny statements like:

"You can get all the justice you can afford"
"Good lawyers know the laws, and Excellent lawyers know the Judges"
"The expression "Honorable Judge" means h*, h*, or many things other than honorable"

On the same time, **WE HAVE GREAT HONEST PEOPLE** in our justice system and the **ratio of good Judges to bad judges is very similar to the ratio of good lawyers to bad lawyers**.

We have a large number of actual court documents that show the **level of corruption, abuse, and the absence of any effective mechanism to correct the system**. People mistrust our legal system, and have **serious issues related to our National Security**. We all know that **fighting corruption is extremely difficult and dangerous**, because the corrupt people build supporters and beneficiaries at the powerful positions **ready to gang together and fiercely fight to the end**. While the people that are willing to fight the corruption are few, not organized, and most of them are reluctant to exhaust their resources in endless fights or long fights to the end. One of the simple things that could help limit the corruption without any cost is to allow the public to do audio and video recording and broadcasting, which most of the courts forbids.

I am very glad that judge Ruth Bader Ginsburg (I don't know if I could say the honorable) made her comments publicly about Trump, which removed the **hidden bias and mask from her face forever**. She provided the undisputed proof about the corruption in our court system I just discussed. She showed the entire world the level of her ignorance and the ignorance of three other judges that shared with her the position to support Obama's unconstitutional order to give amnesty to illegal immigrants. All those four SC judges do not understand the very basic rule that "If any of our laws needs modification, our Congress only can change it. It is unconstitutional and illegal for the president to change any law or its application by any kind of executive order". They proved their bias to whatever Obama does without respect to the constitution. She proved to us how her hidden Burkua made her unable to see the Islamic terror the entire world is witnessing every day. She said; "I can't imagine what this place would be - - I can't imagine what the country would be – with Donald Trump as our president. For the country, it could be four years. For the court, it could be - - I don't even want to contemplate that". She does not need any imagination to know what this place and the country would be. **If she cannot see** what is going on in France, Germany, all Europe, the Middle East, All Africa, Egypt, Saudi Arabia, Qatar, El Bahrain, Pakistan, Afghanistan, - -, and **she did not know about the massacres** of Orlando, San Bernardino, Boston Marathon, - -, I tell her to educate herself and read the facts in this book, then she can have a **better imagination of how the country COULD BE WITHOUT TRUMP**. The political bias, carelessness, and wrong decision of the SC that happened lately in the case of same-sex marriage, which the **four descending Honorable Judges harshly, legally, logically, and rightfully** criticized it against the five majority judges, is the best example for the problems in our SC. I am very happy that the SC took that decision at that time, because it exposed in the best possible ways, the problems that spread into our legal system from its upper top to bottom and from bottom to top. The best part is that the SC decision with the clear opinions of the descending judges that showed unmistakably how the SC went bizarre, are publicly available and I do not need to provide them. The descending Judges said; "Under the Constitution, judges have power to say what the law is, not what it should be". Many judgments at all levels of courts are based on what **should please certain parties**, even if this judgment conflicts completely with other judgments by the same judge.

In my opinion, judge Ginsburg must resign, or forced to resign. All her previous decisions must be reexamined carefully for any improper decisions. It is obvious that the **SC in reality is a political institution not a constitutional court**. We must reform our SC, put term limits, age limits, and **protect it from political appointees and any kind of bias**, to **protect our country and our democracy**.

12. ELECTIONS' REFORM

The current system of election is based on voters selecting a candidate either in a single stage of multi-stages. The proposed system will be based on voting NO and be able to vote Yes, which help deselecting (eliminating) the worst candidates and selecting the best.

The current system in the United States never allowed an independent candidate to win the presidential election in more than two-hundred years, even if the candidate was the best. Many times in the presidential election, voters are to choose between two upsetting candidates. The voting will be mainly based on eliminating the worst and not choosing the best. In such case, the majority of the voters (silent majority) might not vote at all because in their view, both the two candidates are equally horrible.

In electing judges, the majority of the voters do not know anything about them. Bad judges can be elected due to very few voters that can benefit from their elections.

In this proposed system, each voter will vote NO to eliminate who they think is the worst and vote Yes to the best, and then subtracting the NOs from the YESs. So in this way, both these two awful candidates could be eliminated. And we could have been left with the best candidate that did not get many NOs but got few YESs. In the case of judges, the people who knew that this judge is bad will eliminate him.

The great advantage of this proposed system is that it allows the silent majority to cast their votes without going to the polls because if they don't object to certain candidate they have nothing against him or her. While in the current system the people that has objection to certain candidate cannot express their objection to the candidate except by voting to his or her opponent (this opponent could be worse than that candidate). On the same time, it also allows the voters to choose the best after eliminating the worst, allowing an excellent balance between the rejections and the approvals.

13. CLIMATE CHANGE AND JUNK SCIENCE

No one wants to breathe polluted air, drink polluted water or eat polluted food. I believe that the "Global Warming" that started as scientific fact that proved to be wrong, then they changed the name to "Climate Change", indicated that the whole thing is based on junk science. Scientific facts do not change except when you are doing junk science. **It is disastrous to make political decision that impact the economy based on junk sciences**. Amazingly enough, I heard **Obama saying that global warming will make sea level rise by 23 feet**, which I heard from other sources, non of which was able to provide technical data or calculations to support this absurd claim. I was unable to find any scientific model to describe those claimed climate changes that **take into considerations all the factors** that can cause those changes, describe their previous behavior, and predict their future accurately.

I asked a scientist, about this issue and he answered me in a simple and easy way, without a need to go to complicated equations, but it makes all the sense.

He told me that an increase in the surface temperature of the ocean by **3 degrees** centigrade could increase the amount of water vapor by about 20%. This increase of water vapor could reach couple of kilometers above the sea level, which means **tremendous amounts of water evaporation that should reduce the sea level not raise it**. When the air containing high percentage of water vapor cools down (at night), it will generate much higher vacuum (barometric pressure drop), which will move the air at much higher speeds, generating stronger winds and storms with heavy rain (we observed them already). This new pattern of wind will cause changes from the normal rain patterns causing many areas to have unusual rainfalls or draughts. On the same time, increasing the temperature at the north and south poles by 3 degrees centigrade will have a negligible effect on melting ice (its average temperature far below deep freezing). Even assuming that it will melt ice, every one knows that a cub of water having ice when it melt it will not flood the dish, which tell us there will be no volume increase and extremely low rise of sea level. Additionally, there is not enough ice on the north and south poles that after melting can raise the sea level by 23 feet (as Obama believe). The continuous cycle of water evaporation from the sea, to the atmosphere, to rainfall on land, will **continue reducing the sea level**. However, this cycle will reach quickly a balance point where the higher water content in the upper layers of the atmosphere will absorb more the sunlight preventing it from reaching the sea level, which will stop the evaporation.

As for the carbon dioxide generated from fossil fuel, it could go into similar cycle like water vapor. We need to realize that the plants on the earth act as a huge battery. Plants use water, carbon dioxide, and the energy from the sun to form carbohydrates, which cools the earth. Plants grow faster and better at higher temperature, and by storing the sun's energy, it reduces the earth's temperature. These parameters (carbon dioxide generation, absorption, temperature, etc.) will set the conditions at certain balancing points that could be estimated by scientific studies, which I did not see up until now.

Another example of the destructive political decisions not based on solid science, is the attacks on the nuclear energy. Nuclear energy is the best economical and greener source of energy for high demands where there is no cleaner source (as water falls). The amount of dangerous nuclear waste is very small and could be stored safely at relatively low cost.

14.   SOCIAL PROGRAMS

From my personal experience and observations, I recommend the reevaluation of all the Federal and States' social programs, to determine the amounts of the outrages waste and abuse involved in them. It must be clear to everyone that any **government's money** is not the government's money or the politicians' money; it is the **citizens' money**. No one is free to spend it irresponsibly and then <u>**extort the citizens and put his hands in their buckets for more money**</u>.

There are many examples for the ineffective social programs that demonstrate how the workers try to waste time and resources and misinterpret the rules to keep their jobs, and how the citizens abuse the system to avoid doing the right things.

As the excessive spending on many social programs encourage abuse and overload the budget, I recommend limitations, cuts, and modifications to all programs (except healthcare). As an example, programs to help mothers with limited resources and have children, should be as follows:
1.   The financial help should be as loans with low interest rates, and should be non-dischargeable in bankruptcy (like student loans).
2.   The financial help should have limits: per child, per family, and with time limits.
3.   Part of the loan should be the responsibility of the child after certain age (the same idea when good parents work hard and give their children good inheritance and bad parents dissipate their income and leave nothing to their kids).
4.   The governments and the children should be able to sue the parents that misuse the financial help (some parents misuse the financial help for drugs or gambling and let their children live in bad conditions but survive).
5.   Those loans should follow the beneficial everywhere. The government might not be able to collect most of the loans, but at least will be protected from further payments.
6.   Other advantage of this method is that the honest people will not claim that the government is eliminating or cutting their benefits. In addition, the beneficiaries will be more careful in getting the financial benefits and spending them (for example the beneficiaries for housing will not rent expensive apartments relying on the government to pay their rents).

15.   MINIMUM WAGE

The purpose of the minimum wage was to create a minimum standard of living to protect the health and well-being of employees [https://www.law.cornell.edu/wex/minimum_wage]. Therefore, it is to **protect the health and well-being of employees only,** not their families, dogs, cats, or other things. From my point of view, the current Federal Minimum Wage (FMW) is more than enough to give this protection, especially when we apply the healthcare plan proposed above. The FMW issue is **politically dangerous game but economically more dangerous**. We need to remember that the FMW is used to determine many things including the government's social programs to help the low-income families. Increasing FMW will increase those **governments spending** in an already **deficient budget**.

Increasing the FMW will result in the loss or the acceleration of the loss of many of these jobs. Large percentage of these jobs is in fast-food restaurants. These restaurants are working on developing automated systems to: order, pay, and prepare the order at the right moment for pick up, without the need for any human. These systems are in the trial process, however, increasing the FMW will accelerate the development of these systems and make them available to other low paying jobs. Similar results will happen in the manufacturing and the farming industries. Other employers that have to increase the FMW pay will try to increase the productivity of their employees, increase the prices, or reduce the number of employees.

16.   GUN CONTROL

It is a fair and popular demand to eliminate the military style weapons, and severely criminalize their possession and use.

17.   FOREIGN POLICY

Trump is the only one that has good foreign policies. He does not look at Russia as our worst enemy. He respects the rights of the Russian people to live in peace and keep their neighbors friendly.

He understands that Putin has the right and duty to serve his country. Trump wants to reform and develop <u>NATO</u>, which some wise people interpret its name as <u>North Atlantic **Terrorist Organization**</u>. Trump is the only one that tried to keep himself neutral in the Israeli Palestinian conflict. **<u>Trump should support our allies all the time, either right or wrong</u>**. His **<u>support to them when they are wrong is to stop them from doing it</u>**. Our **support to anyone should never be absolute**, those we **support**, must understand that they **need to adhere to the international standards** and our standards, because any deviation from these standards is **<u>very harmful to our reputation, interests, and our ability to support them</u>**. Almost all the dictatorships and terrorist countries are supported by the USA. I strongly believe that **<u>Hillary was not running our foreign policy</u>** during her tenure as the Secretary of State. The **<u>Islamic terrorists were running it through Huma Abdin</u>**, while the **<u>Clintons were busy counting the huge money</u>** coming from donations, speech fees, consultations fees, and revenues from selling the office. Huma Abdin has strong ties with the terrorist organization "The Moslem Brotherhood". Our foreign policies during Obama's presidency were not only a **complete failure**, but also **<u>illegal, irrational, inhumane, discriminatory, and criminal on a very large scale</u>**. It is very easy for any **<u>human (not criminal)</u>** to imagine the reaction of the USA government if the **<u>Syrian government sent weapons or trained fighters to come to the USA to over through</u>** the person occupying the position of the **president**, or even to do legal activities.

The best sad joke I heard lately, was that **<u>Putin of Russia is helping Trump</u>**. I am categorizing most of them as Political Prostitutes. I want to **<u>remind Hillastitutes that ISIS, ISIL, DAESH, Islamists, and illegal immigrants, are continually helping Trump and proving that he was right all the time</u>**.

18.   THE BURKINI WAR AND THE CULTURAL ISLAMIC TERROR

There are storms against the admission of women to the French beaches wearing the Burkini. The Burkini is a swimsuit to cover the body as a Burkaa. **Islamic terrorists**, as always, try to promote this Burkini as an **Islamic swimsuit** for Moslem women to wear on the beaches. The truth is that **Islam's teachings**:

1. **Forbid both men and women from going to beaches where there are women** (almost naked). The **Moslem world never had beaches** where men and women go to swim, except few countries within the last 100 years; it was always a **Western tradition**. This proves that there is **no such thing as Islamic swimsuit**.

2. Forbid women from **going out of their homes generally**, and in case that they needed to go to **respected public places** (Mosques) they must have a male guardian accompanying them. Hence, they are **forbidden from going to beaches**.

3. **Moslem women are not allowed to be in water with men or in front of men, except their husbands only**.

4. Even if we assume that women are allowed to go to the beach with their husbands, I do not think that there is a **respectful Moslem woman** that will let **her husband fill his eyes with the devils** (beautiful women in bikinis), while she is **roasting her self in the sun rapped in this Burkini**.

The entire world, **including Moslems**, know very well that **French beaches** are well known internationally and people from all over the world **come to them for what they offer**. Also, women's **swimsuits are revealing**, which are considered **offending to Islam**. They know that those beaches have their own rules for **admission and dress code. If they do not like these beaches, the way they are, THEY MUST NOT ENTER**; no one will force them to enter, and **there are other beaches all over the world**. Some people try to use silly arguments that if a Christian nun wants to go to the beach, are we going to object. **My answer is YES, we should OBJECT, and the nuns will never call it discrimination or provoke violence**.

In spite of their knowledge of all these rules and facts, **Moslem women go there**?! It is obvious that **they do not go there wearing this Burkini to swim**, relax and expose their bodies to the sun, or enjoy the fresh air, because this Burkini will prevent all these things. The main reasons they go there are to **intimidate, harass, and provoke the French people**. **Certainly, a western woman wearing bikini will be intimidated by the presence of any woman identifying herself as a Moslem in a Burkini or not, knowing that Islam considers just going to the beach is indecent**. **Moslem women wear Burkini to make a very clear and loud statement "You western women are indecent, go and cover yourself or Islam will annihilate you"**.

In reality, this war about the Burkini is not about the **right to get dressed the way you like, or the freedom of expression**, it is the **Moslems' right to insult** and to **subdue western women** and show the **superiority** of Islam. It is about provoking fights, and **destroying the western culture using its civilized laws**. There are many well-known rules: "Eat whatever you like, and **dress the way people like**", and "When you are in Rome **dress like** Romans". **Moslem terrorists are trying to destroy these places and convert them to whatever they want, not to enjoy them**. They are twisting and using the same laws enacted to protect the rights of the citizens (that respect their constitutions) to destroy our public places (**using our laws to destroy us**).

The world could not recognize that during the history of Islam, **Moslems always differentiate themselves from all other religions by their dresses and appearances**. For example, when Moslems invaded and controlled Egypt, they **banned the Egyptians** that did not convert to Islam from doing the following: **wearing clothes similar to Moslems'** clothes, **growing their beards or mustaches** similar to Moslem men, riding horses like Moslems, carrying swords like Moslems, etc. **When Moslems live in non-Islamic countries, they try to differentiate themselves again by not looking or acting the same as the non-Moslems of these countries**, WHICH PROVES THAT THE ENTIRE ISSUE OF THE ISLAMIC DRESSES IS PART OF THE ISLAMIC CULTURAL TERROR.

These Burkini wars, beside the wars about the banning of Burkaa, are <u>part of the Islamic terror against non-Islamic cultures</u>. The world must stand firmly against this <u>CULTURAL ISLAMIC TERROR</u>, and understand its full scope.

19. BERNIE SANDERS

Unfortunately, many people were hoping that Bernie Sanders will stand for them, but he miserably failed them. From the beginning, I noticed his bad judgment, when he could not realize the scale of the criminal actions of Hillary Clinton. He allowed himself to be a moppet for Hillary, to kick his behind and exhibit her lying skills on him as a woman. His standards for honesty were lower than my expectations. An honest person is not only to be honest, but also not to accept dishonest things from others, especially if they direct them against the people he represents. He accepted the corruption in his party, allowed others to play dirty against him and his supporters, and allowed them to show his lack of leadership. As for his wrong stands for the environment, I can excuse him, because it is a fraud imposed upon him and the country. Unfortunately, he could not realize that the people are fed up and angry from the Political Prostitutes in both parties.

20. WE MUST PROTECT HILLARY'S LIFE FOR FUTURE TRIAL

<u>I have a very serious concern that Hillary Clinton could be killed or die by committing suicide, and then blame Trump for</u>

her death. The most probable scenario is that she will commit suicide to avoid the potential trials that could expose her secrets and the secrets of the people that conspired with her, which could uncover her crimes, and eventually put her into prison. My second probable scenario is that her husband Bill Clinton will kill her using the Clinton's expertise in making people disappear mysteriously. Bill's motive will be to hide their crimes and the scandals of the Clinton Foundation. My third probable scenario is that the Moslem Brotherhood (Islamic Terrorists) will kill her due to the failure of ISIS and to cover the support they got from Hillary. My forth-probable scenario is that Obama will kill her, because it is very easy for him to hide the perpetrators, and for all the reasons mentioned in the previous scenarios. We must increase the security for both Hillary and Trump to avoid any assassination trial.

21.   CYBER WAR

Cyber war is the use of the electronic means of communications like the phones and the internet to collect unauthorized information (spying), and hacking into computer systems to: remotely control them, collect secret data, financial transactions, emails, etc. It is not a secret that many countries (including the USA), companies, groups of people, and individuals, are actively trying to develop methods to enhance their abilities in the cyber war, for legitimate and illegitimate reasons.

Crooked Hillary was aware about this cyber war before she became the secretary of state. Lately, she and the Obama's administration declared with certainty that Russia is the country that hacked into her emails, the DNC's system, and is involved in cyber wars against the USA. This declaration raises many **extremely important issues**:

1-   In spite of Hillary's knowledge of the cyber war, she used insecure email system to run the government business, not once or twice, but for all her years in office, and for tens of thousands of emails. This is exactly what I call it **TREASON** (not only extremely carelessness as the FBI director said), in addition to other **criminal consequences**.

2- Crocked Hillary and the Obama's administration, **did not take any action to punish Russia** for this cyber war, or any **effective precautions to prevent any future hacking** like the DNC's email.

3- The **hacking exposed** the DNC's **deception** to suppress the ability of Bernie Sanders to be the party's nominee, reflects **Hillary's deception** and how she **uses gangs to do dirty work** for her, as if she did not ask them to do it, while **she escapes the criminal punishments**.

4- Crocked Hillary's declaration that **Russia is behind** this cyber attacks **without solid proofs** is one of the **most irresponsible actions** that anyone, especially a lawyer, can make.

5- This shows clearly Hillary's and Obama's **lack of good judgment in both their actions of declaring that Russia is the hacker, and inactions of punishment**.

Now, **without feeling any shame** after the discovery of Hillary's email **treason, lies, deceptions, and bad judgments**, she wants the people to **trust her to be a president and control the nuclear switch**! **I do not think that the American people are that idiotic**.

22. OBAMA VETOES 9/11 LAWSUIT BILL

Obama vetoed the bill that would allow family members of 9/11 victims to sue Saudi Arabia. He claimed that the legislation could expose US diplomats and servicemen to litigation in other countries.

Obama is proving again that he is a criminal that must be prosecuted. He is afraid that other countries that were destroyed and the families of the people that were killed due to Obama's SUPPORT TO THE ISLAMIC TERRORISTS are going to be able to sue him. He did not tell us why a country like Saudi Arabia would be afraid of this bill if they did not support the terrorist activities in the USA. He is using the threats of dumping or selling American assets as an excuse. If they do this, the prices of these assets will drop dramatically and other people will be able to win big by buying them at fractions of their values. I hope that they do this.

23. WOMEN, PROSTITUTED MEDIA, POLITICAL PROSTITUTES, AND TRUMP
(October 12, 2016)

The prostituted media gone wild in viciously attacking Trump, hiding the facts and twisting them in every possible way to favor crooked Hillary. One of these attacks was that Trump does not respect women and insults them. To prove this, they used the story of a beauty contestant that Trump told her that she is fat! From my point of view, this story proves how low these prostituted media went down. Let us examine what kind of qualifications these contestants were competing for. For sure, they were not competing for their engineering, scientific, medical, or professional qualifications; they were showing their beauty, or in different words competing for their sexual attraction. The competition has well known standards of weight, dimensions, attractions, etc. When **Trump found** that a **contestant does not meet the standard** of weight, and announced his decision, **Hillary** and the **Prostituted Media, followed by the Political Prostitutes went crying loudly that this is an insult to all women in the whole world**. This shows that they **went lower than any dirty measure for prostitution.**

It is not surprising to see a **flood** of previous **beauty pageants** contestants, and other **similar professions**, coming now accusing **Saint Trump** of all kinds of inappropriate sexual behavior, to harm his chances **against Hillastitutes**. As I said before these women did not come to SaintTrump to demonstrate their engineering skills in building bridges between their tits, erecting rocket launchers to the space, building dams on water passes to generate green or white energy, or explain the scientific basis for global warming caused by women, or to implement their scientific expertise in creating humans from sausage, or their medical skills in exchanging organs, etc., they all came to **market one thing**, which is **their sexual attractions**.

Most of them incurred heavy expenses to come and see Saint Trump, and were all-eager to meet him to **secure** their passage to the **profitable market of beauty**. As in any profession, they **were ready to be examined, tested, evaluated, and tried**. We need to notice that these women do not represent all women, they are very small percentage, and any insult or praise to any one of them **cannot be generalized to all women**. Even assuming that Saint Trump had inappropriate sexual behavior with them **against their will**, why they waited all these years to complain now. The **private life** of a person should never be the subject of a presidential elections, **except** when this person was **holding a public office** and mixed his private life with public work. This is clearly the case for both Bill Clinton and Hillary Clinton, but never the case for Trump. **Trump must sue** everyone that published anything about his **private life or business** either true or false without his permission. Trump must **leave** dealing with these accusations **to lawyers** and **never respond to any** of them either true or false. **Trump needs to focus on the issues** facing the nation, **Hillastitutes crimes**, and the **devastating** impact of a **career criminal** becoming the president of this nation.

We need to notice that **Trump is a private citizen** that his **privacy is protected**, and **no one** has the right to **publish anything about his private life** except with his permission, **even if it is true**. However, Hillary was a public figure and all her actions are subject to scrutiny. Additionally, Bill Clinton raped women, and used government work place and time to commit inappropriate sexual activity, with the **approval and support of Hillary**.

Hillastitutes are the ones that insult **women,** when they consider that **criticizing an imperfection in the sexual attraction of a woman** (her sexual attraction is the only qualification she has**), is an insult to all women.**

Again, it is not a surprise to see **Saint Michelle** Obama join the **Hillastitutes**, she was part of it. Saint Michelle Obama is **criminally responsible** about the killings of the police officers by blacks and is using the same deception like Obama.

24. THE OBAMA'S CASH CRIMES
(October 14, 2016)

It was shocking for many people to know that Obama paid 400 million and then 1.3 billion dollars in CASH to the Iranians, but it was not shocking for me [http://dailycaller.com/2016/09/07/obama-paid-iran-another-1-3-billion-in-cash/] I knew before about him paying the **ousted Moslem Brotherhood president** Mohammad Morsie **billions of dollars in cash to support the Islamic terrorists' activities in Egypt**. **For a president to be able to put his hands on GOVERNMENT'S MONEY IN CASH is the utmost corruption for a president and the system.** What guarantee us that he did not get those millions OF dollars or more, delivered few millions or less, and took the rest for himself and the people that helped him??!! These monies prove to me again that we have a **criminal and gangster in the White House supported by other criminals and Political Prostitutes**.

25. THE ARAB SPRING
(October 15, 2016)

The Arab Spring was actually a grass-root revolution that was stolen by the Islamic terrorists with the support of Hillary, Huma Abdein (Moslem Brotherhood affiliate), and the Obama's administration. This is one of the issues that Trump did not represent it accurately. Trump repeated a statement that does not represent his known morals that the US should have kept supporting Egypt's dictator Hosney Mobarak. The truth is that the Egyptian people revolted peacefully against him after he and his family looted everything in Egypt and destroyed it. At the moment the revolution succeeded to remove Mobarak, a military coup seized the power, and the Egyptian people continued their revolution keeping their peaceful demonstrations, but the terrorist organization of the Moslem Brotherhood (MB) supported by the USA (Obama, Hillary, Huma Abdin, etc.), jumped on the demonstrations shooting the demonstrators and the security forces igniting the killings between both sides. The revolution continued to sacrifice lives and forced the military coup to run elections, in which Ahmad Shafick won against the MB candidate Mohamad Morsie, in spite of the wide spread fraud committed by the MB. However, the MB leaders threatened to flood Egypt with blood if Morsie did not become the president. Again the USA interfered and forced the military coup to declare Morsie as the president. The election committee admitted the fraud, but declared Morsie the winner. After Morsie became president, he appointed his MB terrorists everywhere in the government's positions with full support from the US, which ignited a second revolution under the name "Tamarod", which succeeded in collecting millions of signatures to oust Morsie. Then another military coup lead by General Abdel-Fatah Elsisi seized the power and arrested Morsie. Elsisi enacted a new constitution making Islam the religion of Egypt and Sharia the main source of legislation. Elsisi was elected president in a fraudulent elections (95% of the votes) and injected the military into all aspects of Egypt's civilian activities from building roads, bridges, mosques, hospitals, farming, manufacturing, - - down to distributing infant's milk. His government encouraged the Islamic terror while pretending to fight it, encouraged attacks and discriminations against Christians while pretending to be against them, arrested his opponents, - - etc. He finally threatened and forced the Coptic Church to push the Copts in the US to demonstrate supporting him during his visit to the UN in this September 2016.

The situation in Syria and other Arab countries was much worse than Egypt because the USA was able to support the Islamic terrorists with money, arms, political support, and cover up. Obama and Hillastitutes gave themselves the right to interfere militarily in all those Arab countries to support the Islamic terrorists, and prevent other countries (like Russia) from fighting those terrorists.

26.   COURAGE AND HEROISM
(October 15, 2016)

Obama and Hillastitutes have their own definition of courage and heroism. Oxford dictionary defines "courage" as; "the ability to do something that frightens one" or "strength in the face of pain or grief". While Obama and Hillastitutes consider courage is the change done to someone's reproductive organs, which is private and not the business of anyone, but showing it to the public is courage.

My definition for heroism is; "Someone doing an act to support, defend, or promote a noble purpose knowing that it can cause serious harm or death". According to my definition, I believe that **Julian Assange, and Edward Snowden are heroes**, while John McCain is **not a hero** and I consider him **a criminal**. For Assange, and Snowden, both of them, **exposed their lives and their financials to disastrous consequences for the noble goal** of exposing the corruption and the criminal actions of people and governments, which resulted in several **attempts to kill them by Hillary**, Obama, and others.

As for John McCain, his story was; "On October 26, 1967, McCain's A4 Skyhawk was hit by a North Vietnamese surface-to-air-missile and was upside down and out of control by the time he was able to eject into a lake in the middle of Hanoi." Later he was tortured. [http://www.newsweek.com/sorry-trump-story-john-mccain-war-hero-355617]. First of all, many Americans can agree with me that going and **killing the people** of other countries is **not** by any measure a **noble thing**. Adding to this that Vietnam was not in war, or declared ware on the USA. It is a **cowardice thing the USA was doing and still doing, to kill others because we are stronger and they can not harm us as we harm them**. Second, the fighter jet Skyhawk was at that time, unreachable and relatively safe from the air defenses of Vietnam, hence, their was no certain threat to McCain's life or wellbeing, and even when he was harmed the US government compensated him generously, which is the opposite for Assange or Snowden, no one will care about them. I consider that **McCain is a criminal**, because he supported the **Islamic terrorists to commit their horrendous crimes, and supplied them with weapons and financial support** when he visited Egypt and Syria.
https://www.rt.com/news/220079-mccain-syria-visit-illegal/
http://www.thedailybeast.com/articles/2013/08/06/exclusive-john-mccain-on-his-meeting-with-the-muslim-brotherhood-in-cairo.html

People can evaluate what McCain did by imagining that a similar representative from **Syria visited the USA to meet and provide weapons** to some people that oppose our **dictator Obama**.

27. THE DISASTROUS POLICIES OF CLINTON, BUSH, AND OBAMA

Bill Clinton's scandals and disastrous policies included the Whitewater financial scandal, Travelgate, Filegate, Chinagate (in which he illegally sold our nuclear secrets to China for **campaign contributions for his 1996 election**), and allowed national security breaches at the Los Alamos nuclear facility. He got us into the Bosnia and Kosovo Wars by **lying** that there was genocide in Bosnia and Kosovo (UN courts ruled that there was no genocide). He **aided Islamic terrorists during the Kosovo War**. He **bombed civilians in Serbia** (I saw myself on American TV channel, an American fighter jet, **firing** a rocket at **civilian bus while on a civilian bridge** destroying both, which is clearly a **war crime**). He refused to do anything to **stop the Rwanda's genocide**, and missed many opportunities to capture Osama Bin Laden, paving the way for the September 11, 2001 terrorist attacks.

The Iraqi war was the most disastrous policy for George W. Bush. I was one of the people that **supported the removal** of a **dictator** like Sadaam Hosine, as an **international effort** to establish peace in the world and **avoid the heavy casualties of the wars** that dictators will eventually get their countries involved in them to keep themselves in power. However, once it started, I was shocked to realize that it was an effort of a **super power to destroy a small country to get its wealth** (oil), and get rid of its dictator as a cover-up. The US media **were proud** to announce that our troops were **able to destroy, in few hours, the whole infrastructure** of Iraq including telephone systems, communications centers, bridges, etc. Worst of all, **instead of helping Iraq establish a secular constitution to equate the citizens**; they allowed a faulty constitution that **made Islam the religion of the country, and the Islamic Sharia the main source of legislation**. This was done on purpose, to cleanse the Christians, keep the fighting between the Shiat Moslems, Sunni Moslems, and the Kurds, and to divide the country. Later, the entire world realized that Bush's claim that Iraq was building weapons of mass destruction was a big lie. Even **if Trump supported the Iraqi war** before its start, under the impression that **Bush's** administration has the resources to **know and tell the truth**, then **discovered later**, like me, that this war was a **disaster and retracted his support**, nothing is wrong at all in changing his position. While **Hillary was in a position to know** much more than Trump, but she **supported this war, and continued her support, and now she is admitting that it was just a mistake added to her endless mistakes and lies**.

As for Obama, I mentioned many of his disastrous actions in Ch. 3. The worst of them was **his support to the Islamic terror inside and outside the USA**. He refused to take actions to protect the Christians from the slaughter in the Middle East, and waited until they were cleansed and then moved to **bring the Islamic terrorists to the USA, showing his hate to non-Moslems**.

28. BRITAIN'S EXIT FROM THE EUROPEAN UNION

I am not going to go into details about this issue or try to analyze it as an expert, because I am not. But I can predict, by looking at the whole thing in a logical way, that **Britain will free itself from the damaging rules of the European Union**, and will have **trading relationships** with the countries of the EU **similar to or better than** what was before its exit, and **better relations with other countries**. My reasons are that countries get their position in the world based on their strengths in an open world, while the **countries of the EU are bound with artificial forces** to equate all its members and prevent them from balancing their gains according to their powers.

29.   THE ECONOMY, TRADE AGREEMENTS, JOBS, INDUSTRIAL AUTOMATION, AND WOMEN

I believe that the president of the USA has limited power to improve the economy, but more power to damage it. Because building and developing things take time and resources, while destroying thing could be done quickly and inexpensively.

The secrecy and hiding the negotiations for trade agreements, are signs of the bad intentions of our government, and put the USA in a position worse than an undeveloped country. I believe that we need to negotiate new agreements and renegotiate previous ones taking into considerations the global and local changes. The goals of good negotiations are to maximize our gains without damaging the other side in a win-win setup.

It is a sad joke when the government does not count as unemployed the people that were unable to find work and gave up. We need to keep the unemployment at a minimum. We can do the following actions and steps to reduce unemployment:

1. Implement a healthcare system to give the employee the flexibility to switch jobs and remove its burden from the employers.
2. Bring the manufacturing jobs back to our country.
3. Remove illegal immigrants, and limit the migration to those jobs that we have large shortage in their skills that we cannot compensate for them on the long run.
4. If the previous steps did not achieve the targeted unemployment, then we can reduce the work hours, without reducing the pay per hour, but the total pay could be reduced (not to overburden the employers). For example, with 40 hrs/wk and unemployment rate of 10%, reducing the work hours to 36 hrs/wk (10% decrease) will not reduce the unemployment to 0% but could bring it down to 3% depending on other factors.

We need to remember that when we **bring back our manufacturing facilities**, they **will not generate the same number**

of jobs that were here before. These jobs will be much less due to the automation (for example an electronics assembly facility that was employing 300 for 3 shifts for a total of 900 worker, can run now with only 10 for 3 shifts with a total of 30 worker, a huge reduction to less than 4%). However, they **will bring higher number of high-level jobs**, especially R&D. This tells us that we need to **raise the level of education** to meet the demands for these high-level jobs.

An extremely important element in the economy that people overlook is the role of **women**. I strongly support the right of women to build their families and raise their kids until they reach certain age. However, I do not agree with most of the current laws in these respects. I believe that women need about two years to take care of each of her kids. For example, if a woman planning to have 3 kids and get them after 1.5 year from each, she would need about 5 years to devote herself to them. Having 12 weeks of unpaid leave is not enough; on the same time, increasing it could be very harmful to the employer. One solution is to give women the opportunity to work from home most of the time, which is not available to many jobs. The best solution is to have **low unemployment rate**, which will give **women** the opportunity to **leave work for the time that fits their situation**, and then return to the same job or other one easily.

30. TAX REFORM

I trust Trump to reform our tax code because he dealt with it enough to know many things, he has the experts, and he will do it free from lobbyists and outside pressure for the benefit of the country. However, I want the **medical expenses to be fully deducted** from the income without any limitations and the complications of the current system.

31. ELECTIONS RIGGING AND FRAUD ARE OUR REALITY
(October 20, 2016)

Voting is not the only way to measure the integrity of elections; voting is the last step in elections. Trump does not need to wait to after voting results to declare that the system is rigged, it was already rigged since 2008. The Great Heroes of Judicial Watch proved it in the book "The Corruption Chronicles, Obama's Big Secrecy, Big Corruption, and Big Government", by Tom Fitton, Judicial Watch, July 2012. The book described the harsh reality at that time as:

1. The **liberal media ignored Obama's administration secrecy, corruption, and potentially CRIMINAL acts**;
2. **Corrupt organizations** that are part of the Obama machine's election conspiracy will be **backing Obama with massive amount of money and "volunteers"**;
3. Although **Republicans** will attack Obama for short-term partisan gain, their **own history of corruption** and government secrecy gives no guarantee that they will seriously challenge the underlying culture of the **Obama gang**.

The harsh reality now is much worse than that during 2012. The Prostituted media is running orchestrated attacks against Trump for anything and everything, while ignoring the treasons, crimes, lies, and corruption of Hillary and the Democratic Party. The media with its power is distorting the facts, depriving people from the necessary information to allow them to build good opinions, and destroying any chance for fair elections. Thanks to the **Heroes of Wiki Leaks** for their efforts to expose the **astounding number of corrupt and dishonest people in the media**, and how Crooked Hillary pays them. Additionally, they exposed the corruption in the **entire Democratic Party** and showed how they are **rigging the elections.** Adding to that the inaccuracies in the voting rolls, illegal immigrants voting, voting without ID, dead people voting, etc. We can see that **all the factors that could lead to fair elections do not exist, hence, the CLAIMS that the ELECTIONS are RIGGED are REAL NOW and we do not need to wait to the end of the voting**.

32.   OUR DISASTROUS DEMOCRACY
(October 22, 2016)

The USA is now in a disastrous situation; we have a criminal and corrupt EXECUTIVE BRANCH, criminal and corrupt ATTORNEY GENERAL, criminal and corrupt FBI DIRECTOR, corrupt POLITICIZED SUPREME COURT, corrupt POLITICAL PROSTITUTES, DISHONEST MEDIA, criminal and corrupt PRESIDENTIAL CANDIDATE, and most of the people are MISLEAD and DECEIVED. This is THE GREAT DEMOCRACY that our previous presidents succeeded in establishing during the past 20 years. To perfect this democracy we must bring ISIS to come here, which Obama is actively doing.

33.   CAN HILLARY BE A PRESIDENT
(October 22, 2016)

After all the treasons, crimes, lies, and corruption of Hillary, which are well known all over the world, I cannot imagine **Crooked Hillary** negotiating anything with foreign leaders and **looking at the eyes of each other**. From the polls now (which are rigged), we find that almost **50% of Americans support Crooked Hillary and about 85% of the American and about 95% of the people around the world knows that she is a Crook, LIAR, and CRIMINAL. How a big country like the USA could have a president with these QUALIFICATIONS**.

I believe that the **TRUMP phenomenon**, which is a **patriot to sacrifice** many things and **come forward to lead his government against all the corruption**, is a **historic must**. It happened with Bruce Rauner the governor of Illinois, and **will happen with Donald Trump the president of the USA**.

CHAPTER TWO

ISLAM'S TEACHINGS ACCORDING TO ISLAMIC SOURCES

I was shocked to find many people without any idea about Islam, who established it, at what time, where in the world, and what are its teachings. They just get whatever the prostituted media says as the full truth. Many of those people think that the Islamic terror is not part of Islam's teachings, which is wrong. Some will tell you that other religions and ideologies did worse than Islamic terror, which is wrong to justify certain terror by other terror. Others will say that during the time of the prophet Mohammad terror was the normal nature of war, which is again wrong, because at least Christianity and later Gandhi changed this norm.

I did an academic study, to be used as a reference for the teachings of Islam related to violence, to understand the reasons behind the actions of the Islamic terrors. It is important to disclose the whole truth, not part of the truth, about the teachings of Islam from the original Islamic sources. These sources are the Quran, the statements of The prophet Mohammad (Hadith), and the biography of The prophet Mohammad (Sonna). I avoided using the Islamic interpretations to these sources by Islamic scholars, because Islam considers the text of the Quran and the statements of The prophet Mohammad holy, clear, very precise, and stated in the best linguistic manner (Moslems consider the text of the Quran a miracle that no human or Genie can come close to it), which would eliminate the need for further interpretation. Additionally, the interpretations of Islamic teachings by Islamic scholars conflict with each others, and many Moslems consider most of these interpretations insulting to Islam. I will translate these sources in the most precise way to match the original Arabic text. **Once they are translated accurately, the reader will notice that the <u>meanings are very</u>**

clear and most of the time no further explanations are required, which will help reduce the size of this book substantially.

I will state all the facts with some clarifications whenever needed, **challenging any one to dispute their truthfulness**. I will try to avoid expressing my opinion, but leave every one to build his own opinion according to his standards. Sometimes the reader will notice repetition of many statements from the Quran and Hadith because they could be proving different issues.

To have this part as an academic study, I needed to show and cite the facts and the sources. Unfortunately, the reliable sources that Moslems accept are in the Arabic language, which I know well. From my study of the Arabic sources and their translations, I found these translations not accurate. This made me rely on the original Arabic sources available on the internet. I tried to include the original Arabic references and translate them to my best ability, especially the Quran and the Biography of the prophet Mohammad. The web addresses of these references could be changed, removed, or moved around, and one of those web sites blocked completely my searches. After publishing my first book, the reference showing the miserable situation in Elmadina after Moslems' migration disappeared {http://iucontent.iu.edu.sa}. A reason for this is that, the **careful search will show embarrassing facts that Moslems do not want to show, or they think that it could show harmful pictures of Islam and The prophet Mohammad**. They **deny the existence of these facts**, and say that Jews, Christians, and/or the enemies of Islam invented them. However, when they are finally confronted with these facts, they desperately try to **play with the words, invent stories to justify** these embarrassing facts, try to **find other Islamic statements that contradict them, or pathetically say that since they conflict with recent standards and morals, they should be ignored**. Although ISLAM CONSIDERS THAT ITS TEACHINGS ARE VALID AND MUST BE APPLIED FOR ALL THE SOCIETIES AND ALL THE TIMES UNTIL THE END OF THE WORLD, **they claim that these harmful facts apply only to the time of The prophet Mohammad, which again contradict its teachings and Moslems consider it a blasphemy punishable by death**. All Moslems that they consider themselves Peaceful-Moslems or Moderate-Moslems never studied the teachings of Islam fully; they follow only the peaceful Islamic teachings at the start of Islam before migrating from Mecca. However, when they are exposed to the other teachings after migrating from Mecca, they lock themselves out of the full truth and vehemently refuse to examine them, or change their position. This self-imprisonment is to avoid the Islamic teachings that **punish Moslems who admit any harmful facts about Islam or convert from Islam, by death and the loss of everything**.

The followers of Islam are like the followers of other religions. Some of them follow its teachings very accurately and other followers call themselves Moslems without even knowing enough about Islam. **It is true that all religions claim that the followers of other religions will not go to heaven, however, ISLAM ADDS THAT the followers of other religions SHOULD BE KILLED AND THEIR PROPERTIES, WIVES, CHILDREN, etc. BE TAKEN FROM THEM**. There is no doubt that the **accurate following of the teachings of Islam, do not make peaceful persons, they make terrorists**.

Islam erected huge walls and barriers to prevent Moslems and non-Moslems, from doing logical or academic studies to the Islamic religion. Those barriers included the banning of books, articles, and any materials, that can present harmful pictures of Islam, in addition to assassinating the persons generating or distributing those materials. **A unique feature in Islam is that when you mention to Moslems facts about Islam, they become very angry, accuse you of Islamophobia, insulting Islam, and attack you**. Fortunately, the spread of the internet allowed people to overcome partially those external barriers, but the internal barriers inside the brains of Moslems are still there. There are now many well-respected scholars that did very good academic studies of Islam. I found an article in Arabic, dated 2013/2/9, which is well written and referenced, that all Moslems should read to educate themselves and understand the facts about Islamic terror: http://min-nojoom-alquraan-alkareem.org/articles.php?id=205 Professor Christoph Luxenberg published his study of the Quran in the book "The Syro-Aramic Reading of the Koran", from which one must conclude that the Quran's text had been misinterpreted and misread to an unimaginable degree. Another scholar, Professor Hamed Abdel-Samad (a Moslem worked as a scholar in Erfurt and Braunschweig (Germany)), published many important studies about Islam. His father was a Muslim Sunni Cleric, which enabled him

from knowing Islam very well and studying large number of Islamic references. Most of his works are in Arabic, but many of them were translated to different languages. One of Abdel-Samad's important books is "Islamic Fascism", which was translated to English. He is currently publishing a video series on Islam, under the name "Box of Islam" explaining and analyzing many facts about Islam:
https://www.youtube.com/channel/UCnTJcc901wCa5vZQQot8fCw

Abdel-Samad concluded from his academic research that:
1. **The prophet Mohammad was not a prophet.**
2. **Quran is not a holy book, was copied from other sources, and many times the copying was done in a distorted way.**
3. **<u>Islam is a Fascistic ideology with similarities to the Mafia and Nazism</u>.**

I found an excellent academic author; Dr. Bill Warner. He published many books about Islam. I watched his excellent Youtube video: "**Islam - A Religion Based on Terrorism**", Published on Aug 31, 2012:
https://www.youtube.com/watch?v=t_Qpy0mXg8Y&feature=player_embedded

1. Islam's Different Rules For Non-Moslems

In a society, the people are not concerned about how the followers of a certain religion or ideology practice privately the religious rituals, but they are very concerned about how the followers of a certain ideology deal with others who are different. Islam is unique, because it does not allow its followers to convert from Islam (will be killed), does not tolerate the existence of other religions, and applies different rules to non-Moslems. The application and the following of Islamic rules change according to one permanent rule, which is the Taqyiah, and with the change of the power of the Moslems. When the Moslems are weak, they are peaceful and tolerant, and when they become stronger, they become violent and intolerant. These Islamic rules are stated in the Quran and by example from the actions and words of the prophet Mohammad. Those different rules for non-Moslems cause confusion and misrepresent Islam. To clarify whether ISIL, ISIS, Boko Haram, etc. are following the true Islamic teachings or not, I am going to state some of the facts that highlight the teachings of Islam that were demonstrated by the acts, words of The prophet Mohammad, and supported by the Quran.

IN THE USA, THERE ARE **ANTI-DISCRIMINATION LAWS THAT ARE FULLY ENFORCED**, WHILE IN ISLAMIC COUNTRIES, THERE ARE **DISCRIMINATION LAWS THAT ARE FULLY FORCED**.

Islamic teachings prevent non-Moslems from holding many jobs or positions like judges and leading positions in the government or the army.

In Sharia law, there are many rules that contradict the basic human principles. Moslems do not apply them to themselves but to others. One of these rules is "**All for one**". For example, The prophet Mohammad fought the Jewish tribe of Banu Qaynuqa to **kill all its men** in retaliation **for** the killing of **one Moslem man** (ended expelling the whole tribe). The Islamic story for this is that a Jewish man sexually harassed a Moslem woman, then a Moslem man killed that Jewish man, and another Jewish man killed the Moslem. However, the real reason is that The prophet Mohammad was targeting the Jewish tribes one after the other to get their wealth and properties for his army, as happened later to Bani Koriza then Bani Elnadir.
https://en.wikipedia.org/wiki/Invasion_of_Banu_Qaynuqa

The **best example** for the **discrimination** and **different rules for non-Moslems** imposed by **Sharia-law** is the "**Deya**" (الدية) [defined as the economic compensation to be paid to the family of a killed person for the death of that person], which is **fully dependant on the religion, gender, and freedom status** (slave or not) **of the deceased person**, as follows:

a) If the deceased is a free **Moslem man**, it is paid at **100%**.
b) If the deceased is a free **Moslem woman**, it is paid at **50%**.
c) If the deceased is a free **Christian or Jewish man**, it is paid at **33.3%**.
d) If the deceased is a free **Christian or Jewish woman**, it is paid at **16.7%**.
e) If the deceased is a free **Christian or Jewish man or woman** that their faith was rejected by their communities, it is paid at **00.00% (they should be killed anyway)**.
f) If the deceased is a free man **praying for other God, paying the Gizia, and his safety was guaranteed in a Moslem community,** it is paid at **6.67%**.
g) If the deceased is a free woman **praying for other God, paying the Gizia, and her safety was guaranteed in a Moslem community,** it is paid at **3.34%**.
h) If the deceased is a free Moslem **man capable of fighting but refuse to join Jihad**, it is paid at **00.00% (he should be killed anyway)**.
i) If the deceased is a free Moslem **man or woman that converted from Islam, or does not pray**, it is paid at **00.00% (they should be killed anyway)**.
j) If the deceased is a free Moslem **man or woman that is accused of adultery**, it is paid at **00.00% (they should be killed anyway)**.
k) **If the deceased is a free non-religious man or woman, it is paid at 00.00% (they should be killed anyway)**.

This "**Deya**" rule is a **fundamental one** that Moslems measure on it and expand to other issues.

This rule is the reason that in less than one week in Egypt, Moslems burned and looted about 80 churches and tens of homes of Christians, and killed tens of Christians, without any punishments to the perpetrators or compensations to the victims. Although the Egyptian government knows very well the perpetrators, and there were clear threats, alarms, and many **on-going atrocities**, the **Egyptian government did not take any steps** to **prevent** this from happening, any actions to **punish** the perpetrator, or **compensate** the

Christian victims. The justification is that those Christians are not Christians according to Islam's definition, because they believe that God is Three, hence, they should be killed without any compensation. It should be noted that Egypt has a constitution that affirms human rights, equality, freedom of religion, freedom of speech, etc. All these nice things are thrown out, because the Egyptian constitution states, "Egypt is an **Islamic country**" and "**Sharia-Law** is the main source of legislation".

Now, MOSLEMS are required to explain why this Deya-Rule should not make people ISLAMOPHOBIC.
And why it is NOT in violation of Civil-Rights, Human Rights, Constitutional Rights, Freedom of Religion, and NOT to impose Discrimination, Intolerance, Bigotry, Violence, etc.

THE BEST WAY TO KNOW THE REAL APPLICATION OF THE ISLAMIC TEACHINGS IS TO EXAMINE BY YOURSELF THE SOCIETIES WHERE MOSLEMS ARE THE MAJORITY (like Saudi Arabia, Pakistan, Afghanistan) and

NEVER RELY ONLY ON WHAT MOSLEMS SAY OR TEACH OUTSIDE ISLAMIC COUNTRIES.

2. Islam Interferes With The Enforcement Of The Law

Islam has a very important and fundamental rule that all Moslems are obligated to execute all the teachings of Islam and the statements of the Quran by themselves. This was stated clearly in The prophet Mohammad's statement "Whoever sees something wrong, should correct it with his hands (personally), and if unable (to correct it with his hands) then with his tongue (criticize it vocally), and if unable then with his heart, which is the least for a believer". For example, when the Quran states that the only religion acceptable to Allah is Islam, it is an order for every and all Moslems not to accept any other religion and execute Allah's will, and eliminate all other religions. The entire world is continuously observing this rule in action all the time, either in Islamic or non-Islamic countries. As an example of the application of this rule in an Islamic country; is the brutal killing of a Pakistani Moslem woman by a mob of Moslem men in front of the police, due to an untrue accusations that she burned the Quran. The application of this rule in and outside Islamic countries is shown in the acts of terrorist everywhere. This rule is one of the reasons for what some people say "Self /her Radicalization". It eliminates the role of the law and any chance for anyone to have his/her rights protected, and prevents any fair trials, creating a disorder and chaos in the society.

3. Islam Insults All Other Religions And Criminalizes Them But Would Not Tolerate Any Discussion About Islamic Teachings

At the beginning of Islam when the number of Moslems was small and their power was not enough to force people to join it, Islam showed high standards for Moslems. It accepted: Christianity and Judaism, as Christians and Jews believed; as heavenly religions, the Bible and Torah are Holy Books, and all the previous prophets and messengers of God are real messengers. Further, **Islam made conditions for a person to be a Moslem to believe, respect, and glorify Christianity and Judaism.** It defined a Moslem as "The person who kept people safe from his harm and insults". Islam made it the duty of Moslems to take care of their neighbors and their neighborhood. Islam was tolerant to all non-Moslems including atheists and agnostics. "Say O disbelievers! I do not worship which you worship; nor do you worship which I worship. And I did not worship which you worshipped; nor you are worshipping which I worshipped. You have your own religion, and I have my own religion." [Quran 109:1-6]. "There is no compulsion in religion". [Quran 2-256]. **The prophet Mohammad applied only these teachings when Moslems were weak, which are the basis for some Moslems to claim that Islam is a peaceful and tolerant religion that respects all religions**.

Later when the **number of Moslems became large and their power was enough to force people to join it, Islam reversed its positions completely.** Islam declared that the **Christians**, who believe that Jesus is God's Son, are **polytheistic and disbelievers** that **should be killed and their properties confiscated** ["They indeed are disbelievers who say that Jesus the son of Mary is Allah, Say: Who then can do aught against Allah, if He wished to destroy the Messiah son of Mary, and his mother - - - Jews and Christians say that we are the children of Allah and His beloved people, say: why He then chastise you for your sins, you are humans of His creations - - "[Quran 5:17-18]. "They indeed are disbelievers who say that Allah is the Messiah the son of Mary - -"[Quran 5:72]. "They indeed are disbelievers who say that Allah is a Third of Three - -"[Quran 5:73]. Moslems **should not deal with Jewish people** and avoid them. ["You will find the most vehement of mankind in hostility to the believers (Moslems) are the Jews and the idolaters - - "[Quran 5:82]. "O you who believe! Do not take the Jews and the Christians for friends. They are friends one to another. Who among you that take them for friends is one of them, and Allah will not guide the wrongdoing folk - -"[Quran 5:51]. God's punishment for Jews is to convert them to pigs, apes, and other animals: "... They are those whom Allah has cast aside and on whom His wrath has fallen and of whom He has made some as apes and swine..." [Quran 5:60]; "...You have surely known the end of those from amongst you who transgressed in the matter of the Sabbath, in consequence of which we condemned them: Be ye like apes, despised" [Quran 2:65]; "when, instead of amending, they became more persistent in the pursuit of that which they were forbidden, we condemned them: Be ye as apes, despised" [Quran 7:166]. Jewish and Christians people **should not live in an Islamic society**; they **should leave it or live within Moslems in humiliation**. Islam changed the definition of a **Moslem** from the one that keeps others safe from his harm and insults, to the one that **fights all the non-Moslems to kill them or convert them to Islam (Jihad).** Islam made it the **duty of Moslems to cleanse their neighborhood from non-Moslems**. As I will explain later, although Quran gives the impression that it respects Saint Mary, it talks about her in a way Christians consider it vulgar and insulting; "Your father was not a wicked man nor was your mother a prostitute". [Quran 19:28]. "And Mary - - who guarded her vagina." [Quran 66:12].

Islam claims (without a proof) that the bible is distorted claiming that Christians removed statements referring to the coming of a prophet with the name Ahmed (Mohammad used this name), which Christians consider this as an insult to their Holy Book which refers only to the coming of false prophets. On the other hand, Moslems have thousands of the statements of The prophet Mohammad and of the Quran that they dispute among themselves, and the recent academic studies proved that **Islam's texts had been distorted to an unimaginable degree**.

Islam does not accept the rule "treat others the way you want others treat you". Islam considers itself the utmost and superior true religion while all other religions and ideologies are false that should be eliminated, insulted, and harshly punished. "And whoever chooses a religion other than Islam, it will not be accepted from him, and he will be a loser in the Hereafter." [Quran 3:85].

Following are some additional examples of Islam's insults to others:
1. Quran and The prophet Mohammad describe repeatedly all the non-Moslems, including atheists and agnostics, as **infidels that should be killed and humiliated.** Moslems strongly believe that these are Allah's orders, while all non-

Moslems consider them **not only insults, but also assaults, invitation and provocation of criminal actions**.

2. Quran talks about **Saint Mary** stating; **"Your father was not a wicked man nor was your mother a prostitute"**. [Quran 19:28]. Christians consider this a **vulgar insulting statement** that should have been stated more appropriately as "Your father was an **honorable man** and your mother an **honorable woman**", which is also a **better linguistic expression**. Moslems believe that all the text of the Quran is a miraculous linguistic text that no human, angle, or genie can write anything like it or improve it, and **Allah is praising St. Mary with this vulgar language!!**

3. Quran talks about **Saint Mary** stating: "And Mary - - who **guarded her vagina**." [Quran 66:12]. Again, Christians consider this a **vulgar insulting statement** that should have been stated more appropriately as "And Mary - - who guarded her purity", which is better linguistic expression. Again, Moslems believe that Allah is praising St. Mary with this vulgar language!

4. "Taqyiah" The Principle Of Hiding The Identity And Intentions Of Moslems In Islam

It is worth noting that the word "Taqyiah" is derived from the Arabic word "وقاية" that means protection, not the word "تقوي" that means fearing God. The Taqyiah principle is one of the fundamental rules in Islam. Moslems can hide their intentions, lie about their faith, and even show that they are against Islam, in order to avoid persecution, gain benefits (financial, social, sexual, etc), or surprise their enemies with unexpected or unjustified wars. **Quran, The prophet Mohammad, and the followers of Islam applied the Taqyiah principle extensively in their words and actions**. The Quran, which is assumed to be the words of Allah who knows the past and the future and has the power to do anything, stated the teachings differently according to the power of Moslems. When the power of the prophet Mohammad was weak, the Quran and The prophet Mohammad were peaceful and tolerant to all non-Moslems; "Say O disbelievers! I do not worship which you worship; nor do you worship which I worship. And I did not worship which you worshipped; nor you are worshipping which I worshipped. You have your own religion, and I have my own religion." [Quran 109:1-6]. "There is no compulsion in religion". [Quran 2-256]. When The prophet Mohammad's power increased, the Quran and The prophet Mohammad declared war (jihad) against the disbelievers to eliminate them completely by converting them to Islam, or killing them and looting their wealth and enslaving their women and children. At the beginning, they excluded the Christians and the Jews from jihad (called them the People of the Book or Zumi), gave them some protection, and did not ask them to pay Gizia (protection taxes). This was to neutralize the Christians and Jews to allow the easy defeat of the disbelievers. Finally, when The prophet Mohammad and his followers were able to increase their power, the Quran became explicit in showing the goals of Islam; "And whoever chooses a religion other than Islam, it will not be accepted from him, and he will be a loser in the Hereafter." [Quran 3:85]. **To justify attacking both the Christians and Jews**, the **Quran changed their category from the People of the Book to disbelievers** (Kafer) and ordered Moslems to humiliate them and not to be friendly to them; "They indeed are disbelievers who say that Jesus the son of Mary is Allah - - (17). Jews and Christians say that we are the children of Allah and His beloved people - - (18). O you who believe! Do not take the Jews and the Christians for friends. They are friends one to another. Who among you that take them for friends is one of them, and Allah will not guide the wrongdoing folk - - (51). They indeed are disbelievers who say that Allah is the Messiah the son of Mary - - (72). They indeed are disbelievers who say that Allah is a Third of Three - - (73). You will find the most vehement of mankind in hostility to the believers (Moslems) are the Jews and the idolaters - - (82)." [Quran 5:17, 18, 51, 72, 73, 82]. "**Kill** those who do not believe in Allah, nor in the latter day, nor do they prohibit what Allah and His Apostle have prohibited, nor follow the religion of truth (Islam), out of those who were given the Book (Christians and Jews), until they pay the tax (Jezia) in **submission and humiliation**." [Quran 9:29].

The prophet Mohammad made peace treaties with the tribes under the principle of Taqyiah to neutralize them, until he gained the power to defeat them. It was very easy for The prophet Mohammad to find an excuse to claim that those tribes broke any of these treaties, without resorting to the Quran (Taqyiah), for example by claiming that an Angel disclosed to him their violations. It should be noted that most of the time those tribes were compelled to make those agreements according to The prophet Mohammad's terms, because if they refused to agree, it would mean that they were enemies and had bad intentions.

Quran followed the Taqyiah principle and allowed the Moslems to practice it, and Quran described Allah as the best deceiver and plotter; "Any one who, after accepting faith in Allah, utters Unbelief - except who is forced and his heart is still content with the Faith - On them is wrath from Allah" [Quran 16:106]. "Let not the believers take disbelievers for their friends in preference to believers. Who does that has no connection with Allah, unless it is to avoid harm - - "[Quran 3:28]. "Freedom from obligation (is proclaimed) from Allah and His messenger toward those of the idolaters with whom you made a treaty" [Quran 9:1]. "Allah will not punish you for what is unintentional in your oaths, but He will punish you for what your hearts have garnered" [Quran 2:225]. "And they (the disbelievers) deceived, and Allah deceived them, and Allah is the best deceiver" [Quran 3:54]. "And when those disbelievers plot against you (Mohammad) to wound, kill, or drive you out; they plot, but Allah plot also; and Allah is the best plotter" [Quran 8:30]. "And when people taste Our mercy after adversity which had afflicted them, behold! They have plots against Our revelations. Say: Allah is swifter in plotting, our messengers write down your plots" [Quran 10:21].

The prophet Mohammad encouraged lying, especially for the purpose of wars, and said; "War is a deceit". He made peace treaties with tribes, to neutralize them, knowing that he can claim that they violated it. For example, he made a treaty with Bani-Elnadir to neutralize them in preparation for his coming jihad against all the tribes. Part of it was to help defend the city of El-Madina with The prophet Mohammad when it is under attack. The prophet

Mohammad went outside El- Madina to fight people, and asked Bani-Elnadir for help. They were reluctant to help him, because this war was not to defend the city and outside it. The prophet Mohammad considered this as violation of their agreement. The prophet Mohammad expelled them from their lands for their hesitation. When The prophet Mohammad invaded Khaiber, Hagag Ebn-Alat wanted to go to Mecca to collect his money. He asked The prophet Mohammad a permission to say bad things about him to be able to get his money, and The prophet Mohammad allowed him [Hadith, Elhaithami, Mogamaa El-Zawaed 155/6].

The most **devastating** applications of the Taqyiah rule come from the Islamic teachings **ordering Moslems** to **respect and protect non-Moslems, then** **ordering Moslems to kill and humiliate** non-Moslems.

MOSLEMS USED EXTENSIVELY THE TAQYIAH RULE IN NON-ISLAMIC COUNTRIES TO SHOW THE PEACEFUL FACE OF ISLAM AT ITS BEGINNING, BUT AFTER THEY GAIN ENOUGH POWER, THEY DISPLAY FORCEFULLY THE OTHER DESTRUCTIVE FACES OF ISLAM.

5. The True Moslems Must Follow The Prophet Mohammad As The Best Model

The Quran says about the prophet Mohammad: "You are of a tremendous nature and manners" [Quran 68:4], "We (Allah) sent you as a mercy for the world" [Quran 21:107], and "For the ones that are looking unto Allah and the Last Day, you have the messenger of Allah as a good model." [Quran 33: 21]. Mohammad said that "Allah sent him to complete the best manners". Some Moslems refuse to recognize the teachings of The prophet Mohammad (statements and/or actions) when they feel that they contradict what would be proper teachings. Which means that they deny that Mohammad is a prophet or the Quran is coming from Allah, which in turn subject them to death.

Ironically, some people try to distant Islam from terror and connect it to the teachings of **Salafism or Sonni-Wahabism** only, and claim that there are many other Islamic ideologies that are against terror. These trials **represent deception combined with ignorance**. Deception comes from the factual teachings of Islam as they see in ISIS's actions, and as shown in this book. They are ignorant about the word Salafi (سلفي), which in Arabic means "following the exact teachings and actions of the past generation", which means in Islam: **following exactly the actions of the prophet Mohammad and his companions**. Additionally, the word Sonni (سني) means **following exactly the actions and teachings of Mohammad** (the way he lived, ate, urinated, cleaned himself, had sex, fought, killed his opponents, tortured others, etc.) Both the two expressions Sonni and Salafi mean one thing "**following exactly the actions and teachings of the prophet Mohammad at his time**", without it, no one can claim that he is a true devoted Moslem according to the Quran and Mohammad.
Hence, when people limit ISLAMIC-TERROR to Salafi or Sonni Islam, they are admitting that TERRORISTS are the TRUE DEVOTED MOSLEMS that are following EXACTLY Mohammad's actions at his time.

6. Islam Teaches The Beheading Of The Non-Moslems, Expelling Them, Seizing Their Property, And Taking Their Women And Children As Slaves

After the power of Moslems increased, they expanded their attacks against all the non-Moslems to convert them to Islam. They were giving the non-Moslems (other than Jews and Christians) the choices: 1) be killed; or 2) Become Moslems, while they added to Jews and Christians a third choice 3) paying the gizia. Many tribes rejected these choices, and consequently, Moslems attacked them.

One example was a Jewish tribe, Bani-Koriza. They were terrified by the jihad of the prophet Mohammad (will be explained later), and were forced to agree on a peace agreement with the prophet Mohammad. One of the terms was to support him in defending the city. Mohammad was at war with other tribes, and Bani-Koriza was approached by Mohammad's enemies, but **did nothing against the agreement**. Moslems considered that they had violated their agreement and surrounded and terrified them for about 25 days. Bani-Koriza surrendered as a condition that one of their previous friends, Saad Ebn-Meaaz who had <u>converted to Islam and cooperated with Mohammad, (notice the implementation of Taqyiah in this case</u>) would decide <u>their punishment if any, hoping that he would be fair to them</u>. Saad decided that **all** the adult males to be killed, **all** the women and children to be taken as slaves, and **all** the properties of Bani-Koriza to be taken as spoils of war. <u>Notice that they **were not prisoners of war** and the **punishment was worse than fighting** and it was against **all** and not against the **wrong dowers**</u>. <u>Immediately the prophet Mohammad approved Saad's judgment, saying it is **exactly the Judgment of Allah**</u>. <u>Allah confirmed it also in the Quran</u> "Allah repulsed the disbelievers in their wrath; they gained no good. Allah averted their attack from the believers. Allah is ever Strong, Mighty. He brought those of the People of the Scripture who supported them down from their strongholds, and cast terror into their hearts. You slay some and capture some. And He made you inherit their land, their houses, their wealth, and land you have not stepped on." [Quran 33:26, 27]. The prophet Mohammad isolated the men in one place and the women and children in another place. He ordered the digging of a trench. After that, the prophet Mohammad stood by the trench, and his followers started bringing to him the men of Bani-Koriza, each tied and escorted by guards. In one day, <u>the prophet Mohammad cut off their heads with his sword</u>, and threw their bodies in the trench (some Islamic sources estimated the number of the beheaded men between <u>800 to 1000</u>, while others estimate was <u>600 to 800</u>.) The Moslems seized all the property of Bani-Koriza and took all the women and children as slaves and spoils of war. The Quran came explaining and supporting this story: "You slay some and capture some. And He made you inherit their land, their houses, their wealth, and a land you have not stepped on". [Quran 33:26, 27].

Bani-El-Nadier is another Jewish tribe that Mohammad and his followers attacked without any justification except that Allah told Mohammad that they were planning to kill him. The Moslems surrounded Bani-El-Nadir and started destroying their palm-trees (it is a forbidden action in desert life) to force them into Islam or to surrender. Bani-El-Nadir refused to convert to Islam and preferred to be expelled out from their lands and their ancestors' lands (notice the punishments against **all** the tribe and not against the **ones that planned the purported attack**). Again, the Quran came explaining and supporting the stories of Bani-Koriza and Bani-El-Nadir; "Allah caused those unbelievers from the People of the Scripture (Jews) to go forth from their homes unto the first exile. They thought that they would not go out from their homes, and thought that their strongholds would protect them from Allah. But Allah reached them in an unexpected way. Allah threw terror in their hearts so that they ruined their houses with their own hands and the hands of the believers - -". [Quran 59:2].

Expelling of non-Moslems (ethnic cleansing) is a more lenient way in Islam than killing. Mohammad told the Jews ""If you embrace Islam, you will be safe. You should know that the earth belongs to Allah and His Apostle, and I want to expel you from this land. So, if anyone amongst you owns some property, he is **permitted to sell it**, and otherwise you should know that the Earth belongs to Allah and His Apostle." [Hadith vol 4:392]. http://sacred-texts.com/isl/bukhari/bh4/bh4_396.htm.

7. Any One Who Questions Or Criticizes Mohammad Or Islam Must Be Killed

When the prophecy of any one claiming himself, or people claiming him, as a prophet was challenged or criticized; he proved it

by his good deeds. Mohammad would kill every one who did that.
Mohammad and Quran applied a rule that; any one who criticizes
Mohammad or Islam must be killed, and extended this rule, not only
to the persons doing it, but also to include their families, clans, and
tribes.

Thousands of men were killed for criticizing Islam. For
example, Mohammad sent Salem Ebn-Umir to assassinate a very old
Jewish man: Aabo-Afak, for criticizing Mohammad {
http://en.wikipedia.org/wiki/Abu_'Afak }. Another example,
Mohammad sent five men to assassinate Kaab Ebn-Alashraf.
Mohammad walked them near Kaab, and directed them, and said;
"Go in the name of Allah. Please Allah help them." They went in
their mission, deceived Kaab, killed him, cut off his head, and
brought it to Mohammad {
http://en.wikipedia.org/wiki/Ka'b_ibn_al-Ashraf }.

Although women in Arabian traditions are generally protected
from the killing, many of them were brutally killed. For example, a
high-ranking and well respected old woman, Om-Kerfa, wrote a
poem criticizing Mohammad. Mohammad sent an army to kill her
(the leader of the army was Zaid Ebn-Haretha). Zaid killed many
men in her tribe, and ordered one of his followers (Qayss Ebn-
Elmssaher) to kill Om-Kerfa. Qayss killed Om-Kerfa by splitting
her: by tying her two legs to two camels and moving the camels in
opposite directions, (some Islamic sources mention two horses
instead of two camels). Zaid took Om-Kerfa's daughter and a
young boy (Ebn-Massada's son) and sent them to Mohammad as a
gift, and Mohammad accepted it and praised their killings.
[Ebn-Hisham 617]. { http://sirah.al-
islam.com/Loader.aspx?pageid=326&Words=+%d8%a3%d9%8f%d
9%85%d9%91+%d9%82%d9%90%d8%b1%d9%92%d9%81%d9%
8e%d8%a9%d9%8e&Type=phrase&Level=exact&ID=173987&Ret
urn=http%3a%2f%2fsirah.al-islam.com%2fPortals%2fal-
islam_com%2floader.aspx%3fpageid%3d325%26Words%3d%2b%
d8%a3%d9%8f%d9%85%d9%91%2b%d9%82%d9%90%d8%b1%
d9%92%d9%81%d9%8e%d8%a9%d9%8e%26Level%3dexact%26
Type%3dphrase%26SectionID%3d5%26Page%3d0 }

Another example for killing a woman that criticized Islam is Asmaa Bent-Marawan. She wrote a poem criticizing Moslems for killing people. Although Hassan Ebn-Thabet responded with a poem against her, Mohammad stood among his followers and asked if there is a man that can kill the woman (Asmaa). Omier Ebn-Aady sneaked at night into Asmaa's place while she was asleep among her children and nursing one of them. Omier set aside the child, and stabbed his sword into her chest coming out of her back. He met Mohammad the next morning and told him that he killed Asmaa, Mohammad was **thrilled** and told Omier that the killing of Asmaa **glorified Allah and his Messenger**. Then Omier asked if he would get something for doing that, and Mohammad answered that; no two goats would butt heads for that.

[Ebn-Hisham pg 637] { http://sirah.al-islam.com/Loader.aspx?pageid=326&Words=%d8%a5%d8%a8%d9%86%d8%a9+%d9%85%d8%b1%d9%88%d8%a7%d9%86&Type=phrase&Level=exact&ID=175989&Return=http%3a%2f%2fsirah.al-islam.com%2fPortals%2fal-islam_com%2floader.aspx%3fpageid%3d325%26Words%3d%d8%a5%d8%a8%d9%86%d8%a9%2b%d9%85%d8%b1%d9%88%d8%a7%d9%86%26Level%3dexact%26Type%3dphrase%26SectionID%3d5%26Page%3d0 }

8. Converts From Islam Must Be Killed Or Forced To Become Moslems Again

A person or a group that convert from Islam, are considered enemies of Islam, fighting Allah, and spreading corruption on earth, hence, they must be killed or crucified, or have their hands and feet on alternate sides cut off, or expelled out of the land. In preparation for killing the convert, they isolate his wife and prevent him from spending or dealing in his money. Quran set the punishment for converts at the end of the world; "And who converts and dies in his disbelief: those their works have fallen both in the world and the Hereafter, they will stay in hell fire forever." [Quran 2:217].

Mohammad said, "Whoever changes his religion (convert from Islam) kill him".

An example is the story of Al-Puglieen. Eight men came tired and in need of care to Mohammad's place. He invited them to become Moslems and they agreed, to be safe. Then Mohammad ordered them to drink the urine and milk of camels, which they did. Before the end of the day, they changed their minds and converted from Islam. They escaped very early in the morning and killed the slave that was caring for the camels and escaped by eight camels. Mohammad sent his people after them and they brought the eight men and the camels back to him. <u>Mohammad himself cut off their two hands and two feet, gouged their eyes, and left them to die</u>. Mohammad treated the men this way because they changed their minds and <u>did not believe in him as a prophet or in Islam as a religion, and converted from Islam</u> (<u>Not because they killed the slave, or stole the camels</u>, because killing a slave is compensated for by paying its price not to kill a free person for a slave; and not because they stole the camels because its punishment is cutting off one hand, additionally it is not clear if Mohammad took their camels and horses when they arrived to his camp). The Quran affirmed this punishment after it happened; "The only reward of those who make war upon Allah and His messenger, and endeavor to spread corruption on earth, that they will <u>be killed or crucified, or have their hands and feet on alternate sides cut off, or will be expelled out of the land</u>. That is the disgrace they deserve in the world, and in the Hereafter, theirs will be an awful doom." [Quran Elmaeda 5:33]

Another example is the war against the converts. After the death of Mohammad, all the tribes converted from Islam except Mecca, El-Medina, and surroundings. His successor Abo-Bakr, executed a wide scale brutal war against all the converts, during the years 632 and 633. <u>He killed all the converts that refused to become Moslems, and accepted the ones declaring their adoption of Islam again</u>.

Converts are not only the ones declaring leaving Islam, but also every Moslem that does not follow the teachings of Islam, or the example of Mohammad. This rule was used extensively during the history of Islam, for political and religious purposes to kill and get rid of people and gain more power.

9. Jihad Is a Duty on All Moslems Until the Entire World Becomes Islamic

<u>When Mohammad was spreading his ideas, almost no one believed him, or accepted him as a prophet.</u> Even his wife Aysha did not believe him and said to him; "You have a God that rushes to please you". For example, the <u>whole tribe of Bani-El-Nadir refused to become Moslems, and preferred to be expelled from their lands and leave rather than becoming Moslems. Only two men</u> converted to Islam, Yameen Ebn-Omier, and Abo-Saad Ebn-Wahb, to keep their property, stay, and not be killed. Another example is the eight men that were not convinced that Mohammad is a prophet and did not believe in Islam, so Mohammad cut off their hands and feet and gouged out their eyes.

Mohammad felt rejected, and started to <u>spread his ideas</u> in a way different from any other religion, which <u>he called "Jihad"</u>. For example, Christianity was spread by the good personal model of its followers and explaining its teachings to people and letting them decide for themselves without any pressure. Jihad is simply to use killing and force to eliminate any other religion or ideology (including Islamic teachings that deviate slightly form his teachings), and increase the wealth and population of Moslems.

To attract people to jihad, Mohammad used the four main elements known to attract people to something, these elements are **MONEY; SEX; POWER; and RELIGION**.

At the beginning of Jihad, Mohammad used Taqyiah (deception) to give the impression that Islam supports Judaism and Christianity and is an extension of them. He used the common anti-idolatry to let them think that he is going to fight pagans only. Mohammad enacted peace treaties with Jewish tribes to avoid fighting all of them at once. After Mohammad gained enough power, he and the Quran turned dramatically against Jews and Christians.

Mohammad and his followers did not practice trade or do any other income-generating work like farming. Their **only method of making income** was **Jihad**, which was **attacking** (raiding) the soft targets as **trade caravans**. This way they can get the money instantly. And by converting the people accompanying the caravans to Islam, Mohammad increased the number and power of Moslems, or killing them will eliminate the followers of other religion or ideology. Mohammad and Quran **mandated** jihad **ON ALL FREE-ABLE-MOSLEMS** (who refuses to join Jihad must be killed) all the time, whenever, and wherever there are non-Muslims, until the world's last days; "Fighting is ordained for you, though it is hateful unto you. You may hate something good for you, or like something bad for you. Allah knows but you do not." [Quran 2:216]. Hence, those new Moslems must join the Jihad to increase the wealth and power of Islam.

As for the spoils of war, Mohammad was taking one fifth, but when his followers felt this share to be too large, **Allah took the share** to his name (allocated to Mohammad), and defined the way to distribute it. Quran distributed the spoils of war by dividing it into five shares. Four of the five shares go to the Mojahedin (fighters), and one share goes to Mohammad; "And know that whatever you take as spoils of war, a fifth thereof is for Allah, and for the messenger, the needy close to you, the orphans, the needy, and the wayfarer, if you believe in Allah." [Quran 8:41].

Later Mohammad expanded his Jihad to fight all the tribes and all the non-Moslem people he could reach. It was very easy for him to defeat all those un-unified tribes using his large and unified army. It did not matter if those people were peaceful or not, so long as they were not Moslems, they are legitimate targets. By this large-scale jihad, Moslems were taking the women and children of defeated people as spoils of war, slaves, and sex slaves. Those children and women had no choice but to be Moslems. Quran excludes the women that are spoils of war from the limitation on the number that a male fighter (mojahid) can marry: "And all married women (are forbidden unto you) **except the captives** whom you possess. It is a decree of Allah. It is lawful for you are all beyond those mentioned, so that you seek them with your wealth in honest wedlock, not debauchery. According to your enjoyments from them then give them their payments, but if after the agreement is prescribed, it is not a sin for you to change the payment by mutual agreement, and Allah is ever knowing and wise." [Quran 4:24]. Those women and children will satisfy the sex element, and the power element too, by increasing the number of Moslems. The religious element was used to give legitimacy to this jihad, and to compensate the dead fighters (mojahedin) for what they missed in their lives, by getting it in heaven. Quran explains the things in heaven that they will enjoy; "In gardens of delight; (12) A multitude of those of old (13) And a few of those of later time. (14) On lined beds, (15) Resting therein. (16) There go around them immortal **young boys** (17) with bowls and ewers and a cup of wine from immortal source (18) Wherefrom they **get no headache or bleeding**, (19) And their desired fruits (20) And their desired bird's meat. (21) And women with lovely wide eyes, (22) that looks like hidden pearls, (23) Reward for their deeds. (24) There is no bad words or recrimination (25) but the saying: peace, peace (26). - - And gushing water, (31) And plenty of fruits (32) Neither out of reach nor forbidden, (33) And raised couches; (34) We have created them women a new creation (35) **making them always virgins, (36)** lovers, and friends, (37) to Moslems (38)" [Quran 56: 12 – 26, 32-38]. "Good people will dwell in gardens and delight, (17) Happy because of what their Lord had given them, and saved them from the torment of hell-fire. (18) Eat and drink in health rewarding your deeds, (19) Reclining on ranged beds, and wed to beautiful wives that have wide, lovely eyes. (20) And they who believe and whose generations followed them in faith, We cause their generations to join them, and We deprive them of naught of their work. Every one is a pledge for that which he had earned. (21) And We provide them with their desired fruits and meats. (22) There they pass a cup wherein is neither vanity nor cause of sin. (23) And go around them **young boys** as hidden pearls. (24)." [Quran 52:12–24]. "There (in heaven) go around them immortal **young boys**, when you look at them, you think they are scattered pearls. (19) When you look then you see bliss and high estate. (20). Their upper part dressed in fine green silk and gold embroidery, and silver bracelets, and their Lord gave them a pure drink. (21)." [Quran 76:19-21]. Quran further describes the heaven: "A similitude of the heaven promised for those who keep their duty: Therein are rivers of unpolluted water, rivers of milk that its taste did not change, rivers of wine that bliss the drinkers, and rivers of clear-run honey; therein for them is every kind of fruit, with pardon from their Lord." [Quran 47:15]. "Beautiful women with wide beautiful eyes, detained in tents, prepared themselves and ready for sex (72) - - Whom neither man nor jinni have ever touched - -" [Quran 55:72 – 78}. It is clear that the expressions the Quran used to describe heaven, are very attractive to desert people but not the same for others living around rivers and gardens. For example, water, green, birds' meat, gardens, fruits, rivers, etc. are rare in desert life.

Mohammad used the religious motive extensively, in the form of orders from Allah, or directions from angels. Mohammad said, "I was ordered to fight people until they say no God except one God (become Muslims), and if they say this they gain protection for their lives and properties from me." [Hadith 4:196].

One of the Jihad elements to eliminate the Jews is expressed by Mohammad saying, **"The end of the world would not come until YOU KILL THE JEWS, and the rocks that has a Jew hiding behind it would scream to Moslems**

saying; "here behind me a Jew hiding, come and kill him"." [El-Bokhary].

The people that Mohammad defeated in his wars, he either killed them or offered them to become Moslems and join him and his forces in his fight, giving more power to Mohammad. The men that refused to become Muslims Mohammad killed them, and took their property, wealth, wives, children, etc., as spoils of war.

The Islamic sources themselves give a clear picture of Jihad from the biography of Mohammad. The sources described the actual situation in the areas close to Mohammad. The Encyclopedia of Islamic Books { http://iucontent.iu.edu.sa } describe the following:
The Arabs close to Mohammad were terrified. Whenever they hear that Mohammad is coming to them, they leave their homes and escape to the mountains. The Jews were also terrified, especially after one of them (Kaab Ebn-Alashraf) was killed without justification, and Mohammad made the **killings of Jews** an un-punishable act and part of the jihad (kill the enemies of Allah, Mohammad, and Islam). They could not leave their homes fearing to be killed like Kaab. The Jews complained to Mohammad, and after long discussions, he asked them to have a peace treaty. They were terrified, unable to negotiate, and unable to refuse, so they agreed with humiliation. Mohammad was intercepting the trade caravans going north parallel to the seashore (to Palestine and Syria), which threatened the wellbeing of the tribes that used to use this route. A man, Safwan Ebn-Omyia, stood in a meeting in the tribe of Kuraysh to find an alternative way to keep the trade going. Another one, Alaswad Ebn-Abd-Elmotaleb, recommended using the route to Iraq, which is harsher and longer but away from Mohammad. Safwan prepared a caravan with goods, silver, and gold valued more than 100,000 (one hundred thousand) Derham. One of Mohammad's followers heard about this precious caravan, and rushed to tell Mohammad. **Mohammad sent immediately Zaid Ebn-Haretha in an army (100 men) to catch the caravan as jihad.** Zaid was able to intercept the caravan at a place called Alkerdah. The men of the caravan left everything and escaped. Zaid captured the whole caravan and two owners of the goods (one

of them was Forat Ebn-Hayan). Zaid returned to Mohammad with these **precious spoils of jihad-war**. Mohammad took one fifth of the spoils (as Allah ordered), which was about **20,000** (twenty thousand) Derham, and divided the rest to that army of Mojahidin (each got about **800** (eight hundred) Derham). The captured man, Forat, was offered to choose between death or become Moslem, and he chose Islam, but **did not get any of his goods back**. Notice the big difference between the share of a fighter (Mojahed) [800] and Allah's share that Mohammad took [20,000], which is much larger than the normal.

{ http://sirah.al-islam.com/Loader.aspx?pageid=326&Words=%d8%a8%d9%86%d9%8a+%d8%a7%d9%84%d9%86%d8%b6%d9%8a%d8%b1&Type=phrase&Level=exact&ID=45040&Return=http%3a%2f%2fsirah.al-islam.com%2fPortals%2fal-islam_com%2floader.aspx%3fpageid%3d325%26Words%3d%d8%a8%d9%86%d9%8a%2b%d8%a7%d9%84%d9%86%d8%b6%d9%8a%d8%b1%26Level%3dexact%26Type%3dphrase%26SectionID%3d5%26Page%3d1 }.

Other Islamic sources mentioned this story of capturing this valuable trade convoy as a "Jihad War", under the name Alkerda war. {http://sirah.al-islam.com/Page.aspx?pageid=204&BookID=160&TOCID=474}.
         This story gives a clear picture for the reality of Islamic Jihad. Mohammad considered that a valuable caravan going away from his men, is a declaration of war that mandates Jihad and whatever captured from this Jihad are lawful spoils of war that Allah will get his share, and forcing a captured man to become Moslem is the ultimate Jihad.

         Using Allah as a religious element to justify and order Moslems to the jihad is evident from a huge number of Quran's statements. Notice that, after doing all the killings Allah is forgiving and merciful. Here are some Quran's statements: Allah like those who fight in unity [61:4]. Take and inherit the wealth, property, women, and boys of non-Moslems; "And He brought those of the People of the Scripture who supported them down from their strongholds, and cast terror into their hearts. Some you slew, and some you made captive. (26) And He caused you to inherit their land and their houses and their wealth, and land you have not trodden. Allah is ever able to do all things." [33:26-27]. The best assurance for a Moslem to go to heaven is through fighting for the cause of spreading Islam (Jihad) and being martyred; "And if you are slain, or die in the way of Allah, forgiveness and mercy from Allah are far better than all they could amass". [Quran 3:157]. Motivate Moslems to jihad; "O Prophet! Exhort the believers to fight. If there be of you twenty steadfast they shall overcome two hundred, and if there be of you a hundred steadfast they shall overcome a thousand of those who disbelieve. because they (the disbelievers) are a folk without intelligence." [8:65]. Kill them; "And **kill them until persecution is no more, and religion is all for Allah**. But if they cease, then lo! Allah is Seer of what they do." [8:39]. "Those who believe do battle for the cause of Allah; and those who disbelieve do battle for the cause of idols. So kill the minions of the devil. Lo! the devil's strategy is ever weak." [4:76]. "So kill in the way of Allah Thou art not taxed (with the responsibility for anyone) except for thyself - and urge on the believers. Peradventure Allah will restrain the might of those who disbelieve. Allah is stronger in might and stronger in inflicting punishment." [4:84]. **Cut off the heads of the disbelievers**; "When you meet the faithless, **strike their necks**. When you have thoroughly decimated them, bind the captives firmly. Thereafter either release them or take ransom until the war lays down its burdens. That (is Allah's ordinance), and had Allah wished He could have taken vengeance on them, but that He may test some of you by means of others. As for those who were slain in the way of Allah, He will not let their works go awry." [47:4]. "Let those kill in the way of Allah who sell the life of this world for the other, whose killing in the way of Allah, be he slain or be he victorious, on him We shall bestow a vast reward." [4:74]. "Kill them! Allah will chastise them at your hands, and He will lay them low and give you victory over them, and He will heal the chests of folk who are believers." [9:14]. "O you who believe! Kill those of the disbelievers who are near you, and let them find harshness in you, and know that Allah is with those who keep their duty (unto Him)." [9:123]. "Kill in the way of Allah, and know that Allah is Hearer, Knower." [2:244]. "Mohammad is the messenger of Allah. And those with him are harsh against the disbelievers and merciful among themselves." [48:29]. "The only reward of those who make

84

war upon Allah and His messenger, and endeavor to spread corruption on earth, that they will <u>be killed or crucified, or have their hands and feet on alternate sides cut off, or will be expelled out of the land</u>. That is the disgrace they deserve in the world, and in the Hereafter theirs will be an awful doom." [5:33]. "Then, when the sacred months have passed, <u>slay the idolaters wherever you find them, and take them (captive), and besiege them, and prepare for them every ambush</u>. But if they repent and establish worship and pay the poor-due (become Moslems), then leave their way free. <u>Allah is Forgiving and Merciful</u>." [9:5]. "<u>O Prophet! Strive hard against the disbelievers</u> and the hypocrites! Be harsh with them. Their ultimate abode is hell, and evil is their destination." [9:73]. "Allah has bought from the believers their persons and their property for they will be in heaven. They <u>kill in Allah's way, so they slay and be slain</u>. It is a promise binding on Him in the Torah and the Gospel and the Quran; and who is more faithful to his covenant than Allah? Rejoice therefore in the pledge which you have made; and that is the supreme triumph."[9:111]. "So **do not falter and ask for peace when you are the uppermost**, and Allah is with you, and He will not waste your deeds." [47:35]. "The <u>religion for Allah is Islam</u>. Those who (formerly) received the Scripture differed only after knowledge came unto them, through transgression among themselves. Who disbelieve the revelations of Allah, Allah is swift at reckoning." [3:19]. "And <u>whoever desires a religion other than Islam, it shall not be accepted from him</u>, and in the hereafter he shall be one of the losers."[3:85]. "Kill those who do not believe in Allah, nor in the latter day, nor do they prohibit what Allah and His Apostle have prohibited, nor follow the religion of truth (Islam), out of those who were given the Book (<u>Christians and Jews</u>), <u>until they pay the tax (Jezia) in submission and</u> **humiliation**." [9:29]. "Prepare for them all the armed forces and of horses tethered, to dismay the enemy of Allah and your enemy, and others beside them whom you do not know, but Allah knows them. Whatsoever you spend in the way of Allah it will be repaid to you in full." [8:60]. "Kill in the way of Allah against those who fight against you, but begin not hostilities. Allah does not love aggressors. (190) And <u>slay them wherever you find them, and drive them out of the places</u> whence they drove you out, for persecution is worse than slaughter. And do not fight them at the Mesged El Haram until they attack you, but if they attack you then slay them.

Such is the reward of elkaferin (disbelievers). (191) But if they desist, then <u>Allah is Forgiving, Merciful.</u> (192) And <u>kill them until persecution is no more, and religion is for Allah (Islam)</u>. But if they desist, then let there be no hostility except against wrong-doers. (193) ."[2:190 –193].

<u>Mohammad ordered every Moslem to **fix what he sees wrong by hand (force)**, and if he could not then by his tongue (words of criticism), and if he could not then by his heart, which is the least (for a believer).</u> { http://hadith.al-islam.com/Page.aspx?pageid=192&BookID=25&PID=141 } This Rule <u>conflicts with the role of governments in any civilized society</u>. It allows every Moslem to apply his own interpretation of what is wrong according to the teachings of Islam, which have a very wide range of judging the same thing from an extreme right to an extreme wrong, especially **JIHAD (Quran said Jews are good people, and also; Jews are infidels, and enemies of Allah, and must be killed and eliminated)**.

With jihad, Moslems became very rich and powerful very quickly.

10.   The Real Nature Of Jihad

As explained before, the battle of Alkerda was a Jihad war to intercept a precious trade caravan of expensive goods, gold, and silver, worth more than 100,000 Derham. The Moslems' army captured it with two of its owners without any resistance or hostile action against Moslems. The Moslems took it all without giving the owners anything, even after converting to Islam (against the rule that whoever converts to Islam will have immunity from confiscating his property).
{ http://sirah.al-islam.com/Loader.aspx?pageid=326&Words=%d8%a8%d9%86%d9%8a+%d8%a7%d9%84%d9%86%d8%b6%d9%8a%d8%b1&Type=phrase&Level=exact&ID=45040&Return=http%3a%2f%2fsirah.al

-islam.com%2fPortals%2fal-
islam_com%2floader.aspx%3fpageid%3d325%26Words%3d%d8%
a8%d9%86%d9%8a%2b%d8%a7%d9%84%d9%86%d8%b6%d9%
8a%d8%b1%26Level%3dexact%26Type%3dphrase%26SectionID
%3d5%26Page%3d1 }.
{http://sirah.al-
islam.com/Page.aspx?pageid=204&BookID=160&TOCID=474}.

The real nature of Jihad was to wage continuous wars to attack others, irrespective of them fighting the Moslems or not, and gain the spoils of these wars under the name of Islam. These continuous wars were the only job that Mohammad and his followers had. They **recruited others by force**, or by attracting them to **share the spoils** of these wars. As I stated before, **JIHAD IS SIMPLY TO USE KILLING AND FORCE TO ELIMINATE ANY OTHER RELIGION OR IDEOLOGY** (including Islamic teachings that deviate slightly form his teachings), **and INCREASE THE WEALTH AND POPULATION OF MOSLEMS**. This is exactly what ISIS is doing.

11. Islam Does Not Tolerate The Existence Of Non-Moslems

As I mentioned before, at the beginning of Islam when the power of Mohammad and his followers was small, he and the Quran were tolerant to people of other religions "There is no compulsion in religion"[Quran 2-256]. They were also peaceful with Christians and Jews (calling them the People of the Book), gave them some kind of protection, and **did not ask them to pay gizia** (protection taxes). "And do not argue with the People of the Scripture unless in a better way, except the unfair ones. Say: We believe in what was revealed unto us and revealed unto you; our God and your God is One, and unto Him we surrender." [29:46]. Then turned against Jews with praising Christians "You will find the most vehement of mankind in hostility to the believers the Jews and the idolaters. And

<u>You will find the nearest of them in affection to the believers the Christians</u>." [5:82].   Later, when Mohammad and his followers were able to increase their power, they started to attack both the Christians and Jews, and categorized them as disbelievers, enemies of Allah, enemies of Islam, Moshrekeen, etc. [Quran 5:17, 18, 51, 72, 73, 82]. "They indeed have disbelieved (kafer) who say Allah is the Messiah, son of Mary." [5:17]. Quran forbids Moslems from dealing with Jews and Christians; "O you who believe! Do not take the Jews and the Christians for friends. They are friends one to another. Who, among you who takes them for friends is (one) of them. Allah will not guide the wrong doers."[5:51]. "Those of the Children of Israel who became disbelievers were cursed by the tongue of David, and of Jesus, son of Mary, because they rebelled and were transgressors."[5:78].

There are conflicting teachings in Islam, especially when it comes to treating the non-Moslems, which changed from being peaceful at the start of Islam to becoming terrifying at the end. Some scholars consider them as a clever application of the Taqyiah rule, while Quran explains them as rewriting and improvements of those teachings. "**Whatever versus We abrogate or cause to be forgotten, We bring (in place) one better than or like it. Do you not know that Allah can do anything**". [Quran 2:106]. In reality, those improvements are dramatic changes of the teachings of the Quran and Mohammad, from being pleasant to Jews and Christians, to declaring war against them, by categorizing them as disbelievers, enemies of Allah, and enemies of Islam that should be killed. They were an application of the Taqyiah principle. Those changes had a devastating effect on Jews and Christians. It resulted in the elimination of them from the Arabian Peninsula, and reduced their numbers dramatically in the countries that Moslems invaded. In addition, these changes were used according to the whims of Moslems. For example, **if they wanted to get the support of the Christians, they can tell them that Islam is friendly to Christians according to the teachings of Quran and Mohammad.** However, when they **want to attack the Christians and seize their properties, they accuse them of being disbelievers according to the teachings of the same Quran and the same Mohammad.**

Ironically, the **Gizia** is a protection-tax to **protect non-Moslems from the Moslems** themselves not outsiders. <u>Moslems disarm and forbid non-Moslems from carrying weapons to protect themselves to humiliate them and keep them under Moslems control (notice the similarity to **Mafia**)</u>.

Islam considers itself the superior religion and Allah does not allow other religions; "The religion to Allah is Islam - - (19), - - And whoever desires a religion other than Islam, it shall not be accepted from him - - (85)." [3:19,85]. Even if there are non-Moslems within a Moslem majority, they should be treated with humiliation as second and third class citizens, pay taxes, and be isolated. Mohammad prohibited Moslems from staying with non-Moslems
{ http://sirah.al-islam.com/Loader.aspx?pageid=326&Words=%d8%a8%d9%86%d9%8a+%d9%82%d8%b1%d9%8a%d8%b8%d8%a9&Type=phrase&Level=exact&ID=19002&Return=http%3a%2f%2fsirah.al-islam.com%2fPortals%2fal-islam_com%2floader.aspx%3fpageid%3d325%26Words%3d%d8%a8%d9%86%d9%8a%2b%d9%82%d8%b1%d9%8a%d8%b8%d8%a9%26Level%3dexact%26Type%3dphrase%26SectionID%3d5%26Page%3d0 }.

<u>Mohammad ordered Moslems not to start saluting Jews or Christians, and if they meat one of them on the road, to force them to its narrowest part.</u>
{ http://sirah.al-islam.com/Loader.aspx?pageid=326&Words=%d8%a8%d9%86%d9%8a+%d9%82%d8%b1%d9%8a%d8%b8%d8%a9&Type=phrase&Level=exact&ID=15564&Return=http%3a%2f%2fsirah.al-islam.com%2fPortals%2fal-islam_com%2floader.aspx%3fpageid%3d325%26Words%3d%d8%a8%d9%86%d9%8a%2b%d9%82%d8%b1%d9%8a%d8%b8%d8%a9%26Level%3dexact%26Type%3dphrase%26SectionID%3d5%26Page%3d0 }.

A Moslem may not be killed for killing an infidel (non-Moslem).

Moslems should not take orders or guidance from non-Moslem "O you who believe! if you obey those who disbelieve, they will make you turn back on your heels, and you turn back as losers". [Q 3:149].

Moslems should not take Jews or Christians as friends "O you who believe! Do not take the Jews and the Christians for friends. They are friends one to another. Who, among you who takes them for friends is (one) of them." [Q 5:51].

Moslems may lie and deceive non-Moslems "Let not the believers take disbelievers for their friends in preference to believers. Who does that has no connection with Allah, unless it is to avoid harm - - ." [Q 3:28, 29].

Mohammad said that at the last day, for every Moslem that dies, Allah would sacrifice a Jew or a Christian (push them to Hell) to make the Moslem go to heaven, even if his sins are heavier than mountains. {Sahih Moslem, Ketab Altoba, part 4}. Although the text of this statement is very clear, and many approved Islamic sources confirmed it, Islamic scholars try to explain it in a way to reduce the impact of its terrible teachings. They contradict it by other statements of Mohammad, which again proves that his statements and teachings are conflicting. Islam is unique in that you can find justification for doing many things and their opposites at the same time from its teachings.

The hatred to Jews and the desire to kill and eliminate them from Islamic societies and from the whole world, is evident from the orders of Allah to Mohammad "**The end of the world would not** come until **YOU KILL THE JEWS, and the rocks that has a Jew hiding behind them would scream to Moslems saying; "here behind me a Jew hiding, come and kill him"**." [El-Bokhary].

Moslems sometimes say that Islam allows the marriage of Moslems to non-Moslems, which is not true. **Moslem men only can marry non-Moslem women and their children must be Moslems**, while **Moslem women are completely forbidden from marrying non-Moslems** (a Moslem-woman marrying non-Moslem husband is considered convert and must be killed). Also, if a wife became Moslem, her kids must become Moslems, and her husband must become Moslem or divorce her (thankfully not to be killed).

12. Islam Does Not Tolerate The Existence Of Other Moslems

Islam is not only intolerant to non-Moslems; but also is intolerant to other Islamic thinking. This intolerance is not in the form of rejecting and arguing against that thinking, but it is killing those who think differently. Since I want to focus this book on the facts that most of the people do not known well, because of the lack of references, and since the history books discussing those killings are readily available, I will be very brief to reduce the size of this book. Those killings, started when Mohammad had enough power to fight and force his ideas, which continued to these days and will continue in the future, because Islam prevents its followers from the critical thinking. The **history of Islam shows clearly intolerance, hatred and brutal wars and repeated massacres by Moslems against other Moslems and against all non-Moslems**. The majority of those wares and massacres against other Moslems, were between the Shiite and Sunny, which is witnessed by the whole world and many historical references are filled with their details. As another example, the Ahmadiyya (Moslems believing that other prophets will come after Mohammad, are regarded by many other Muslims as non-Muslims and "heretics") are systematically attacked violently in Pakistan. Recently the **massacres against the Yemenis**

91

by Saudi Arabia and its allies, with the help of the USA, demonstrated Islam's hostility to others. Notice that Yemenis did not commit any hostile act against Saudi Arabia, but **being a Shiite Moslem is enough justification to be killed by Sunni Moslems**.

13.   Women In Islam

In the previous editions of this book, I did not try to examine how Islam treats women. I was affected by the way I was raised in an Islamic society, and considered this issue to be an internal family matter not a public one. However, I found that western countries and the USA consider it a very important public issue, and they enacted tough laws in this respect. Additionally, I found a big **propaganda** with many misrepresentations **that Islam respected women and their rights**. The simple fact is that Islam considers women as properties of men, and women are less intelligent and not equal to men. Most of the time, Sharia treats a **woman's worth as half that of a man**.

Following is some of the ways Islam and Sharia Law look at women:

1- Mohammad stated that all women are deficient in their brain and religion, and their guile is very great.
http://www.moheet.com/2014/03/09/2024032/%D8%AA%D9%81%D8%B3%D9%8A%D8%B1-%D8%B1%D8%A7%D8%A6%D8%B9-%D9%84%D9%84%D8%B4%D9%8A%D8%AE-%D8%A7%D9%84%D8%B4%D8%B9%D8%B1%D8%A7%D9%88%D9%8A-%D9%84%D8%AD%D8%AF%D9%8A%D8%AB-%D9%86%D8%A7%D9%82%D8%B5.html#.V14lNzGrF3A

2- Some Islamic scholars consider the statement " - - this is of the guile of you women, your guile is very great." [Q 12:28] could be applied generally to all women.
http://fatwa.islamweb.net/fatwa/index.php?page=showfatwa&Option=FatwaId&Id=146601

3- A woman's Deya is half that for a man (woman's value is half of a man), which I discussed before.

4- The testimony of a woman is half of that of a man. For example, if a woman was raped by a man without witnesses, and the woman testified that that man raped her while he denied that rape, she will be considered a liar and could be stoned to death, which happens frequently in Islamic countries (punishing the victim of rape not the rapist).

5- A Moslem man can marry up to four women at the same time, in addition to having unlimited number of sex slaves [less than what Mohammad had; https://www.thereligionofpeace.com/pages/quran/muhammads-sex-life.aspx]. However, a woman cannot marry more than one man even if this man is married to many women. If a woman is married to more than one man, she will be considered adulterer that should be stoned to death.

6- A Moslem man can kill all the men in the family of a non-Moslem woman and marry (rape) her on the same day (Mohammad killed the father, brother, and husband of a newly married woman, her name is Safia [her father was Haay Ebn-Aghtab, the leader of the tribe of Bani-Elnazir], and Moslems consider that this marriage was the highest honor that Safia could get).

7- Men are in charge of women and should beat them if they disobeyed them. The best description for this is stated in the Quran: "**Men are in charge of women**, because Allah made some **preferred than the others**, and with the **money they spend on them**. So **good women are the contented ones**, guarding the absence - - - as Allah guarded. As for those from whom you **fear rebellion**, **admonish** them and **banish them to beds** apart, and **scourge them**. Then if they obey you, do not seek a way against them." [Quran 4:34]. Notice that a man is not required to wait for a woman's rebellion to materialize, just fear of this rebellion is enough to act without delay. In Western countries if a man beats his wife he could be imprisoned.

8- Normally the power to divorce is given to husbands. However, in rare cases, the wife might have this power by stating it in the marriage-contract, which could be a sign of bad intentions from the woman. When men have the power to divorce, they can divorce their wives at anytime without a reason, and the wife can get all her divorce rights like alimony, custody of minor children, etc. On the same time, the wife cannot divorce her husband except for valid reasons and by special Sharia panel (institution), which could be a difficult and long exhaustive process. In case that this Sharia panel finds that the wife has no valid reasons for divorce, she could be denied the divorce, and her husband can force her to live in his house or in an "Obedience House". According to Sharia, the requirements in this "Obedience House" are minimal. Any livable space without luxury items could be good enough. For example, it could be a tent with carpet to sleep on; billow; cover, and toilet. Lately, Islamic countries realized that the "Obedience House" is practically a private prison for wives. They tried to abolish it or distant Islam from it, in spite of the actions of Mohammad and the clear statements in the Quran [4:34].

The most important factor in subjecting women to Islamic rules (Sharia), is that **women must obey these rules to their extremes**. When a woman deviates from Sharia, **even in her belief**, her guardian (father, husband, brother, or son) will have an immediate duty to **force her to change her mind** or face punishments that could vary from torture to death.

In Islam, a woman is something that has no ability even to think for herself, or make reasonable decisions.

14. Homosexuality In Islam

The issues of homosexuals (LGBT) in Islam, is another example of the issues that I did not give them the attention they deserve and ignored to mention them in my earlier copies of my books. Part of this was due to the way I was raised in an Islamic society, where these issues are not considered human rights issues. All Islamic countries have severe laws and rules against the homosexuals, and most of them make death as the punishment for homosexuality.

Quran made it clear that Allah will punish the homosexuals: "What! men have sex unto the males, and leave the wives your Lord created for you? Nay, you are dreadful people. They said; if you Lot did not cease doing it, you will soon be of the outcast. He said; I hate your conduct, my Lord! Save me and my household from what they do. Therefore, We saved him and his household all. - - . Then afterward We destroyed the others, and We rained on them dreadful rain because they have been warned. This is indeed a portent, yet most of them were not believers." [Quran 26:165-174]. Mohammad also said that Allah will curse the men that imitate women and the women that imitate men [El Bokhary]. Adding to these statements that Islam's teachings obligate Moslems to execute Allah's wishes to their maximum abilities, which give the individuals the right to attack the homosexuals and apply Allah's curses and kill them.

 Islamic scholars agree that the **penalty for homosexuality is death**, but they differ in the way of execution. They recommend **throwing them from the highest building, imprisoning them in a dirty rotten place to die, stoning them, cutting off their heads, using a sharp wedge,** etc. As I said before, the best way to know the facts about Islam's position towards an issue is to see how Islamic countries apply it like Saudi Arabia, Iran, Pakistan, Afghanistan, etc. **In the case of homosexual's rights, it is clear that Islam's teachings are against them in contrast to the constitutions and laws of countries like the USA or western counties.**

15. Moslems Promote And Teach Islam Hiding Its Full Reality

Moslems who studied Islam, especially the ones that will teach Islam, are well aware about its troubling teachings. They cannot deny these teachings or they will be killed, hence, they have to hide its full reality according to the students and the societies. For example, when teaching Islam in Islamic countries, where all the students are born Moslems, they teach people the full real Islam with its violent teachings. In non-Islamic countries, like Europe and the USA, we have two kinds of students: the children of Moslem families (Moslems by birth), and the non-Moslem citizens (students). In both cases, they hide those troubling teachings, and teach the students only the peaceful teachings at the beginning of Islam. After learning those peaceful teachings, all the Moslem students will love Islam more and become trapped in Islam and willing to accept and adopt any extreme or radical teachings, and then they might continue their education in Mosques where they learn the real Islam. As for the non-Moslem students (citizens), they will be impressed by these peaceful teachings and will like Islam and defend it thinking that they learned the real Islam.

It is the responsibility of the western countries to

TEACH ITS PEOPLE THE FULL REAL TEACHINGS OF ISLAM, **as they are stated in the Quran and from the actions and statements of Mohammad, and PRACTICED AND APPLIED IN ISLAMIC COUNTRIES**.

16. How and Why Moslems Become Radicalized

If Islam's teachings were only the peaceful ones, no one could have had a problem with it, but no one could have considered it a new religion or considered Mohammad a new prophet, because these teachings were copied from the teachings of Christianity and Judaism. This was the real problem for Mohammad when he started his message, people did not consider him a prophet, ignored and harassed him, and eventually forced him and his followers to leave Mecca and migrate to Elmadina. Mohammad started a new **violent phase** after the migration, which people describe it these days as **"Radical"** after seeing the actions of ISIS (as if they discovered something new). Mohammad used extreme violence to spread his message by wars, eliminated any criticism or questioning of his methods by killing whoever dared to discuss them, and protected his army and society from collapsing by killing any one who would think about leaving Islam. This radical phase is Islam's final development and utmost teachings. When devote Moslems fully study Islam, they will end being radicalized.

Following are the **steps, Moslems go through them, explaining how and why they end up being radicalized**:
1) Learn the peaceful teachings of Islam and they like it.
2) Convince themselves that Islam is the best religion.
3) Brain-wash themselves to erase their brains, and reject any idea to study it in a logical way, and use its teachings to verify it (for example, they use the statement of the Quran "You are of a tremendous nature and manners" [Quran 68:4], to prove that Mohammad had good manners, without examining his unjustified killing of 1000 men of Bani-Koriza, or cutting off the two hands, two feet, and gouged the eyes of the 8 men that converted from Islam).
4) Become devote Moslems, which require them to learn Islam deeper, practice it, obey it, and execute its teachings at the utmost level, which is jihad.
5) Do the Islamic prayers regularly to avoid the death penalty for not practicing them.
6) Join Jihad to avoid the death penalty for not joining it.

RADICALIZATION IS THE END RESULT OF MOSLEMS FOLLOWING THE FULL TEACHINGS OF ISLAM AND AVOIDING

17. The Similarities Between The Migration Of Moslems From Mecca To Elmadina And The Migration Of Moslems to Western Countries

It is a fact that the **people in both Mecca and Elmadina were tolerant to all religions**. Mohammad started spreading his massage in a peaceful manner in Mecca, but very few people were convinced and the majority rejected his ideas. After the death of his first wife, he lost her support, and the people of Mecca started harassing him. Mohammad and his followers migrated to Elmedina, which he chose because of its strategic location with respect to trade routs and for the peaceful and tolerant nature of it people. After migrating to Elmadina, Mohammad planned and executed the building of a very strong army to spread his Jihad. He started by inviting El-Saalik to join Islam (El-Saalik were groups of gangs formed from the men that escaped and hide from their tribes; to avoid punishments for crimes they committed; and were making living by attacking others and escaping with whatever they can get) [https://nihaiatulislam.wordpress.com/tag/%D8%A7%D9%84%D8%B5%D8%B9%D8%A7%D9%84%D9%8A%D9%83/]. Mohammad offered them God's forgiveness, and a share in the spoils of Jihad. They accepted his offer and joined him, which was the first step in building an army from professional brutal fighters. After a short period, the situation in Elmadina changed completely, and the peaceful enjoyments of the tribes, especially the Jewish tribes, were completely reversed. The migration to Elmedina gave Mohammad the opportunity to build his army, eliminate the Jewish tribes, and to prepare to invade Mecca.

This is similar to what we see now in **Europe and USA, where Moslems benefited from the tolerance** of these societies to

98

spread Jihad, increase their power, and terrify any one that might think about doing any thing Moslems consider it against Islam. Also, Moslems migrate to other countries to spread Islam the same way Mohammad did.

18.   ISIL's Point Of View

According to all the analysis given before, we can realize that ISIL represents the real Islam, and considers itself the real devoted Moslems. All other Moslems that we call, or they call themselves, Moderate Moslems, ISIL considers them infidels and converts from Islam that according to the teachings of Islam itself must be "killed or crucified, or have their hands and feet on alternate sides cut off, or will be expelled out of the land" [Quran 5:33].

Most Moslems all over the world know that ISIL is following the real teachings of Islam, and support them. Many studies were done to measure the opinion of people in Islamic countries (Turkey, Pakistan, Afghanistan, etc), and found huge numbers of the people do not consider ISIL as terrorist organization.

It is impossible for 2,000 or even 50,000 fighters of ISIL, to swiftly seize large areas with large populations in Iraq and Syria, without the support of local Moslems.

We must **be careful when we decide to fight ISIL**, because the fight will **not be limited to ISIL's fighters**, but to **ALL THE MOSLEMS THAT SUPPORT ISIL and its ideology INSIDE AND OUTSIDE ISIL's territories**.

19.   Are There Moderate Moslems?

From the previous study, we find that there is only one Islamic teaching and its followers are the real Moslems, and any other religion or thinking are strictly prohibited and should be eliminated. The prime minister of Turkey (Erdogan) said it clearly and simply, when he said that "Islam is Islam without any modifier". Hence, there is no modifiers, or such things as Moderate Moslems, Fanatic Moslems, or Extremist Moslems. No one was able to give the definition of "Moderate Moslems". Are those the Moslems that apply the (peaceful) teachings of Islam at its beginning which were later changed by the Quran and Mohammad? Or those that does not follow the violent acts of Mohammad? Are those Moderate Moslems the ones that try to interpret the Quran against its original text to cope with the developments of human standards? All these things are **strictly and explicitly prohibited by Islam itself** and considered heresy punishable by death. Those Moderate Moslems are non-Moslems, but keeping themselves under Islam to avoid the death penalty to themselves and their families. They are trying to live in peace, hoping that they can stay this way indefinitely.

One of the basic characteristics of humans is their ability to freely express themselves in a civilized manner. Even if we assume that, there are Moderate Moslems that differ in their interpretation of Islamic teachings, and adopt what could be a moderate Islam, their silence for what they oppose, would not qualify them to be called Moderate Moslems. Additionally, if they oppose the terror of Jihad, they are attacking Islam, therefore they are converts and non-Moslems, that devote-Moslems must kill them, eliminate them, and make them disappear, which eventually make them **non-existent**. Hence, we come again to the same conclusion that in the world of Islam, **Moderate Moslems does not and CAN NOT EXIST**.

20.   Are There Extremist Moslems or Radical Moslems?

From the previous study, and from the way people talk about radical Moslems, we can have a better definition for extremist or radical Moslems. **Radical Moslems are described as those who kill, loot the property, and enslave others that do not follow the teachings of Islam as those radicals apply them**. One of the characteristics of Islam as Moslems believe is that its text is holy, perfect, precise, and coming from Allah. No one should ever change a single character in its text, and it is forbidden to translate it to any other language to avoid the loss of the exact meanings of its text. Before we analyze the Radicalism, we need to notice two important words in the Arabic language and the Quran. The first word is "harb حرب ", which means "war", for the use of force (could be deadly) to impose the will of one side on the other. The second word is "ketal قتال ", which means "kill" for the killings of the enemies to eliminate them and impose the will of one side on the other. The Quran very rarely uses the word "war" to order his followers to do jihad or anything (I cannot recall stating war for one time in the Quran for the purpose of achieving Islam's goals). However, it uses the word "killings" to achieve Islam's goals all the time, as demonstrated from the large number of Quran's statements mentioned before. As an example for the use of "killings" and "war", the Quran states: "The only reward of those who make **war** upon Allah and His messenger, and endeavor to spread corruption on earth, that they will be **killed** or crucified, or have their hands and feet on alternate sides cut off, or will be expelled out of the land." [Q 5:33] This demonstrates clearly the use of the two words "war" and "killings", and show that when **someone wages war against Moslems or Islam, the response should be killings not war**.

Radical or extremist describes someone who interprets a statement that could mean many things from extreme left to extreme right. However, when a statement has only one clear and precise meaning, there is no room for radical, extremist, or moderate interpretation. It is only what it is and whoever follows this statement is the rightful, faithful, and devoted follower and not an extremist or radical. Examining the actions of those radicals as stated above, we find that they follow precisely the statements of the Quran and the Prophet Mohammad. Following are some actions of Mohammad and statements from the Quran calling for the killings of non-Moslems:

1. The Prophet Mohammad **cut off the heads of about 1000 men by himself with his sword** (Bani-Koriza massacre) [he untruthfully accused them of violating their peace agreement and held them as prisoners of war].

2. **Mohammad cut off** the two feet, two hands, and gauged the two eyes of eight men that converted from Islam.

3. "When you meet the faithless, **strike their necks**. When you have thoroughly decimated them, bind the captives firmly. Thereafter either release them or take ransom until the war lays down its burdens. That (is Allah's ordinance), and had Allah wished He could have taken vengeance on them." [Quran 47:4]

4. "And **kill them** until persecution is no more, and religion is all for Allah." [Quran 8:39]

5. "So **kill in the way of Allah**." [Quran 4:84]

6. **"Kill them! Allah will chastise them at your hands."** [Quran 9:14]

7. "O you who believe! **Kill those of the disbelievers** who are near you, and let them find harshness in you." [Quran 9:123]

8. **"Kill in the way of Allah**, and know that Allah is Hearer, Knower." [Quran 2:244]

9. "Then, when the sacred months have passed, **slay the idolaters wherever you find them**, and take them (captive), and besiege them, and prepare for them every ambush." [Quran 9:5]

10. "Allah has bought from the believers their persons and their property for they will be in heaven. **They kill in Allah's way**, so they slay and be slain." [Quran 9:111]

11. **"Kill those who do not believe in Allah**." [Quran 9:29]

Everyone knows that, the history of Islam shows clearly that when Moslems waged wares, they took the properties of the defeated and took their wives and children as slaves. The Quran also ordered Moslems to do that as a gift from Allah; "And He brought those of the People of the Scripture who supported them down from their strongholds and threw terror into their hearts. You slay some and capture some. And He made you inherit their land, their houses, their wealth, and a land you have not stepped on". [Q 33:26, 27].

Even if we assume that the number of radical Moslems is less than 0.1% (it is more than 70%), it means that there are more than 1,100,000 terrorists that can cause destruction more 55,000 times the 911 attack, which is 165,000,000 deaths.

This analysis above confirms repeatedly that ISIS is following precisely the teachings of Islam, considers itself the real devoted Moslems not radical or extremist Moslems, and challenges everyone to prove otherwise.

TO ALL THOSE WHO SAY THAT ISLAM IS A RELIGION OF PEACE OR THAT ISIS OR ISIL IS NOT ISLAMIC, EXTREMISTS, RADICALS, OR ANY OTHER DESCRIPTION; OR SAY THAT THERE ARE MODERATE ISLAM, THEY ALL HAVE THE BURDEN OF DISPUTING THE ABOVE ANALYSIS AND PROVING THEIR CLAIMS FROM THE FULL TEACHINGS OF ISLAM ITSELF NOT BY JUST MAKING UNSUPPORTED STATEMENTS.

They also have the burden of showing that moderate-Moslems are not a negligible small number of people who call themselves Moslems without knowing the core teachings of Islam, and without any effect or enforcement for what they claim to be moderate-Islam.

21. Can Moslems Integrate In Western Countries Or The USA

All Moslems, whatever you call them: moderates; terrorists; radicals; or peaceful, and irrespective of their level of education as highly educated; or illiterate, have at least the following common things among themselves:
1) Sharia law must be the law of the land, if a Moslem does not believe in this; he is not a Moslem and must be killed.
2) Anyone who criticizes Islam must be punished harshly, which is against the freedoms of religion and expression.
3) Any Moslem who leaves Islam must be punished harshly, which is again against the freedom of religion.
4) Islam is the superior religion.

Any Moslem, who does not believe in the mentioned four things, is considered non-Moslem and should not be counted as a Moslem.

It is easy for people from different countries to migrate to western countries, enrich their culture, enjoy what they offer of human rights and dignity, become citizens that respect their constitutions, and integrate themselves in those countries. However, it is very difficult for Moslems to integrate themselves in western countries because Islam's teachings are incompatible with their constitutions or the human rights they protect. Moslems would not accept, respect, or willing to obey those countries' constitutions. Moslems consider western countries corrupt, indecent, and immoral, and the ways women are dressed in them are forms of nudity. The people in nude societies do not force others to join, and they welcome others to come and join according to the rules of their nudity, while Nuns and fully dressed people are not welcomed, and no one will call this discrimination or complain about it. No one in those **immoral societies forced Moslems** to go and live there, it is the **failure of Islamic societies** to provide them with the **minimum human rights**.

Moslems go to western countries to live according to Islam's rules and laws, not the well-established rules and laws of those countries, and they end up clashing with those societies and isolating themselves. The main clashing issues are:

1. <u>Freedom of religion</u>: Western countries define the freedom of religion as the ability of anyone to practice, study, analyze, compare, criticize, choose, and join or leave any religion, without pressure, fear, or discrimination. However, <u>Islam's definition of freedom of religion is completely the opposite, it is the **freedom of Moslems to criticize, criminalize, insult, etc. all other religions** and force people to become Moslems and **kill them when they leave Islam**</u>. Moslems use slogans like; "Do not insult Islam, and we will not insult your religion", or "Do **not insult** Islam, so that we do not **kill you**". Western countries do not give special treatment to any religion or discriminate against any. They consider religions as ideas subject to all kinds of discussions without violence. They could not put a standard to measure what could be an insult because of the conflicts between religions. For example, Quran states that Christians are infidels that should be killed, while Christians rely on the Bible to prove that Mohammad is a fake prophet, which Moslems consider it an insult. Hence, western countries decided not to put any standards or punishments for insulting ideas, and left <u>every idea to **defend** and protect itself by **peaceful discussions**</u>. Ironically, Moslems try to **force** the entire world to use the **Islamic standards** in defining what is an insult to a religion [e.g. saying that Christians are infidels is not an insult] (Please refer to chapter 2 above). Islam's definition of insults to Islam is very wide and could include almost anything. For example, the female Islamic scholar "Aisha Abdel Rahman", published an academic study about Mohammad's wives that she was able to document, Moslems considered it insulting to Islam and wanted to kill her. Another example, Moslems consider **an Insult to Islam the stating of the facts**: that Mohammad **cut off** <u>the two hands, two feet, and gouged the two eyes, **of eight men**</u> because they **converted** <u>from Islam;</u> and the **fact that** <u>Mohammad himself, without any justifications, **cut off the heads of about 800 men**</u> from Bani-Koriza, and took all their women, children, and properties as spoils of war. In addition, a minor discussion to reform the interpretation of some teachings of Islam could be considered an insult to Islam.

2. Freedom of expression: Moslems consider Islam a political, financial, and social systems enacted by Allah, and valid for all times and all societies. Any modifications, changes, or criticism to any of them, are considered insults to Allah and Islam and are forbidden. Hence, **no one is free to express** or discuss any views that **disagree** with Islamic ones. [Historically, there are many situations when the follower of Mohammad had to **deviate** from clear statements in the **Quran**, which prove that its teachings are **not valid** for all times and societies].

3. Women's rights: Every one can see the huge differences between women's rights in Islam and in western countries. Moslem men and women alike do not waste any opportunity to display those differences, which show the superiority and the decency of Islam. They even succeeded in bringing Sharia courts with its bias against women to many places, sometimes under the disguise of family matters, in spite of violating the common laws in these places, and women's rights. One of the displayed differences on women's rights is the Islamic **dresses for women**, which western people consider them **symbols of abuse**, while Moslems consider them **symbols of decency** and criticize the western dresses for women as forms of nudity, and describe western societies as immoral, indecent, and "Nude Societies". If Moslem women did not wear the Islamic dresses, no one will notice them and they will integrate themselves in the societies. There is an international saying "eat whatever you like, but dress like others". However, most Moslem women and their male guardians insist on wearing the Islamic dresses to distinguish themselves, intimidate western women, and **declare that their religion is Islam**, which could be used as a **reverse discrimination** and **blackmailing** tool, by claiming that they were targeted because they are Moslems. **Certainly, a western woman wearing western dress will be intimidated by the presence of a woman in Islamic dress**.

4. Superiority of Islam: As Moslems believe that Islam is the superior religion, they believe that they should not integrate in other non-Islamic societies, but other societies must disintegrate into their system.

5. Sharia law: As explained before, Sharia is against the basic human rights and incompatible with the western's constitutions and systems, and it is a fundamental element to be a Moslems. We can observe the success of Moslems in establishing many Sharia courts in many western countries. Hence, there is no motive for them to integrate and abandon their Sharia. They can wait to have enough power to **change those constitutions to be compatible with Sharia**, which will be the **disaster for those countries that they deserve**.

6. Anti discrimination laws: As explained before, Islam's teachings brutally discriminate against non-Moslems, giving Moslems the impression that they are superior. They have no motive to integrate and go down from their superior position to equate themselves with other citizens.

7. Minorities rights: I showed before that in Islam there are no rights for non-Moslems, which applies automatically for all minorities. In some cases, minorities should be eliminated, like Christians, Jews, Yazidees, homosexuals, etc.

8. Using violence to force their ideas: Western democratic countries have well established systems to allow citizens to do changes in their societies using peaceful means. They forbid the use of coercion or violence to make these changes. During the history of Islam from its start until these days, Moslems used violence to spread and impose Islam's teachings. Current violence is displayed in the actions of ISIS inside and outside western countries. A country like France, where the number of Moslems is high, was a good place to display the Islamic violence in forms other than cutting-off heads, or the recent massacres that were executed by relatively small number of people. One of these violent actions; is the display of Islam's power by **huge number of Moslems** living in France; when they **gather** from many places **into one place** in an **open display of power and to intimidate the residence** of this place, by **fully blocking the streets during Friday's prayers**. Although it is illegal to block the streets and the police should arrest whoever does it, the **police officers** become **scared** and **unable to enforce the law**. Another form of violence in Islam is provoking others to be violent. A good example of this is when **Moslem women go to French beaches wearing burkini** (Islamic swimsuit covering the whole body). They know very well that on those beaches women's swimsuits are revealing, which are considered **offending to Islam**. They know that those beaches have their own rules for **admission and dress code**, if they do not like them they should not enter; no one will force them to enter. Also, in **Islam, women are not allowed to be in water with men or in front of men**. In spite of their knowledge of all these rules, **Moslem women go there**?! It is obvious that they do not go there to swim, relax and expose their bodies to the sun, or enjoy the fresh air, because this burkini will prevent all these things. The main reasons they go there are to intimidate, harass, and provoke the French people. Those beaches are known internationally and people come to them from all over the world for what they offer, and now Moslems are trying to destroy these places and convert them to what they want. Additionally, The world needs to stand for these kinds of Islamic harassments and intimidations.

9. Islam does not accept the freedom of choice: All societies are built on the principal "**Live as you want, and let others live as they want**". In Islam, it becomes "**Live as Islam demands you, and kill and die to force people to live as Islam wants**".

10.Moslems raise their children in Islam not in the host country: I hosted a young girl (about 10 years old) from France in a student-exchange program about 20 years ago. At the beginning, I did not know that she is a Moslem and her parents were originally from Algeria. I was shocked to find out that she was raised with deep hatred to France, Christians, Jews, non-Moslems, and her community. It is no surprise to see the Islamic brutalities devastating France after those children were raised on hate.

The problem is that the USA and western countries are **afraid of discriminating against Moslems, knowing that Islam is incompatible with their systems and constitutions, and discriminates against all non-Moslems. Their politicians, either ignorant politicians or Political Prostitutes, adopt policies that allow Moslems to come to their countries, knowing that Moslems will never integrate in their societies**. They leave their countries to suffer from the consequences of these incompatibilities. On the other hand, **Moslems benefit from these policies and use them as a first step to conquer these countries.**

22.   Obama's And Other Moslems' Misleading Comparison Between Christianity And Islam To Justify The Islamic Terror

I avoided in this book comparing Islam with other religions or ideologies. However, I found that Obama like some Moslems made many misleading comparisons and statements about Islam and Christianity, which I need to discuss. Even if we assume that his statements were true, he should be ashamed of trying to justify a twenty first century's terror, with a seventh century standards.

On 9/24/14, Obama said, "Christianity endured centuries of vicious sectarian conflict. Today, it is violence within Muslim communities that has become the source of so much human misery. It is time to acknowledge the destruction wrought by proxy wars and terror campaigns between Sunni and Shia across the Middle East." There are huge differences between Christianity and Islam in the violent acts of their followers. There is nothing at all in the Bible that exhorts Christians to be violent or to kill others, or makes the killing of non-Christians a guaranteed way to go to heaven. While the Quran, Mohammad, and the teachings of Islam, all have huge number of teachings to exhort Moslems to kill non-Moslems and make the killing of non-Moslems a guaranteed way to go to heaven. Jesus said,"And if <u>anyone hears my words and does not believe, I do not judge him</u>; for **I did not come to judge the world but to save the world**." [John 12:47]. While Mohammad said, "I was ordered **to fight people until they** say no God except one God (**become Muslims**), and if they say this they **gain protection** for their **lives and properties from me**." [Hadith 4:196]. In addition, the Quran is filled with huge number of statements to kill the non-Moslems, I previously included some of them, but as a reminder, here is one example "<u>slay the idolaters wherever you find them</u>." [Quran 9:5]. The facts are clear, Christianity is peaceful but the evil nature of people makes them violent, while the teachings of Islam are evil, which make its followers violent.

Obama then stated that "Today, it is violence within Muslim communities - - - wars and terror campaigns between Sunni and Shia." These wars and terror did not start these days; it started after the death of Mohammad, and continued until today and will continue in the future, until all Moslems realize the truth. The real nature of Islam was affirmed after the death of Mohammad when the Moslems themselves killed Mohammad's <u>cosine, his only daughter, and his two only grand sons</u>. This raises a **big question** that Obama and every Moslem needs to answer, which is:
<u>Can a real devote peaceful Moslem kill Mohammad's cosine and grand sons</u>, if that Moslem really believed that <u>Mohammad is really</u> the <u>Messenger</u> of Allah, and that the <u>Quran is Holy coming from Allah</u>????

On "National Day of Prayer" (February 5th, 2015) Obama said, "And lest we get on our high horse and think this is unique to some other place, remember that during the Crusades and the Inquisition, people committed terrible deeds in the name of Christ. In our home country, slavery and Jim Crow all too often was justified in the name of Christ." [http://www.whitehouse.gov/the-press-office/2015/02/05/remarks-president-national-prayer-breakfast]. Obama basically reminded Christians not to get on a moral high horse in their harsh criticism of the ISIS atrocities because the Crusades and slavery were also justified in the name of Christ. Mainly, he tries to justify ISIL's atrocities comparing them to the atrocities of Christians. Although his statements are shocking in their misrepresentation, he clearly exposed his inside.

There are similarities between the Crusades and ISIL, but not in the way Obama meant. ISIL created recently a terrifying situation in the region similar to the terrifying situation in Jerusalem around the year 1065. In 1065, the Moslem Turks took Jerusalem by force, massacred over 3000 Christians, and treated the remaining Christians very badly.
[http://thecrusadesinformative.weebly.com/essay.html, http://www.medieval-life-and-times.info/crusades/, http://www.lordsandladies.org/cause-of-crusades.htm]
The Crusades was a normal response to stop the atrocities committed against Christians and to release the Holy Land from the Islamic terror. Similarly, Obama himself is asking the whole world

to stand for the atrocities of the Islamic terror, as the (Christian) countries did during the Crusades, but he is just talking without any effective actions to stop the brutality of ISIL, **while preempting international efforts waiting for the lead of the USA**. On the other hand, there are huge differences between ISIL and the Crusades, which I explained before many times. There is nothing in the bible to suggest or justify the Crusades, while Islamic teachings are the main motive for ISIL.

Obama in his misleading statements pointed to the excessiveness of the Christian Spanish Inquisition, and accused Christianity of justifying slavery. Both these statements are false and none of them has any support whatsoever in the Christian teachings. On the other hand, the teachings and history of Islam show clearly the excessive violence against the non-Moslems, and other Moslems that differ in their views, and the enslaving of women and children.

Many people claim, "**all religions** went through **violent periods in their history**", and Islam is not an exception. This is **not true**; the truth is that "**all human societies went through violent periods in their history**" (Separate religions from the actions of people). **Religions** that consider themselves heavenly religions; Judaism, then Christianity, and then Islam, should **represent civilized development from one to the next**.

We can observe that:

    a) Judaism's teachings have:
1- Some violent teachings;
2- Its followers are the "Chosen" people that are superior to others.
3- Not every one can joint their religion.

    b) Christianity came as a development to Judaism:
1. **eliminated all violent** teachings to move humans towards a much **better peaceful civilization.**
2. **Equated** all humans.
3. **Invited** all people to **join** it and **enjoy its peace**.

c) Islam should have been a development to Christianity; instead:

7. Its **teachings became extremely violent.**
8. Considered itself the **Superior religion** and all other religions **must be eliminated.**
9. Practiced the **utmost discrimination** against non-Muslims.
10. **Used extreme violence to force people to join it**.

After the people realized the importance of the freedom of religion and established the principle of "Separation of Religion and State", they were able to establish much more civilized societies. However, **Islam's teachings do not allow the separation of the government and Islam**. We can see easily, that most of the Moslem-majority countries have the first statement in their constitution "The country is Islamic". Although a country is not a person that can practice the religion, which makes this statement meaningless, but they insist on stating it and other religious statements (like: Sharia-Law is the main source for legislation), to emphasize the mingling of the State and Islam, and re-emphasize the discrimination against non-Moslem citizens. The separation of religion and state, allowed the followers of a religion to reject and/or modify some teachings of that religion without fearing for their lives, while Moslems are not allowed to reject and/or modify any teachings of Islam, because they will be considered enemies of Islam that must be killed. Moslems are simply trapped in Islam, if they try to leave Islam they will be considered converts that must be killed, or if they stay Moslems and try to modify the Islamic teachings to avoid its violence they will be considered altering Allah's teachings and enemies of Islam that must be killed. This will close the door for them to join any non-Islamic society that does not allow violence. Because if they truthfully denounced the violent teachings of Islam to be compatible with the system relying on its peaceful teachings at the beginning of Islam, they will become non-Moslems because the violent teachings came after the peaceful ones to erase and replace them (considered improvements).

Again, the facts are clear; Christianity has peaceful teachings, but the violent nature of some people makes them act violently, while the teachings of Islam are violent, which make its followers more violent. However, NOT ALL MOSLEMS

ARE VIOLENT, BUT ALL MOSLEMS ARE POTENTIALLY VIOLENT AND MUST BE TREATED ACCORDINGLY. We can also say that the Muslim people are not different compared to other people, hence the problem we need to face is not the Muslims, it is the VIOLENT TEACHINGS OF ISLAM THAT CONTRADICT ITS PEACEFUL TEACHINGS (at the start of Islam when it was weak).

Now let us summarize and reemphasize the following:

NOT ALL MOSLEMS ARE VIOLENT, BUT ALL MOSLEMS ARE POTENTIALLY VIOLENT AND MUST BE TREATED ACCORDINGLY.

THE PROBLEM WE NEED TO FACE IS NOT THE HUMAN MUSLIMS; IT IS THE VIOLENT TEACHINGS OF ISLAM AND ITS FOLLOWERS.

23.   The Effect Of Taqyiah Principle

The Taqyiah principle in Islam, makes every Moslem a **hidden bomb** waiting to explode at an **unexpected** moment and conditions, even if this Moslem is really a peaceful person. All the people that dealt with the terrorists that executed the 9/11 attack,

113

said that they never thought that any one of them could do, or could have the intention to do, this terror. The Boston Marathon bombers gave the people that new them the same peaceful impression. The Taqyiah principle is devastating to the democratic and civil societies. <u>Democracy, allows people to express their views freely in a civilized peaceful manner, without fear or a need to hide them,</u> **eliminating the need for Taqyiah**. Democracy allows every one to change the society peacefully to what he wants by convincing the majority that this change is good for them. In addition, the Taqyiah is extremely dangerous for the law and order. Imagine a neighborhood with normal population of Jews, Christians, Atheists, etc. and one Moslem person goes to live there to execute his Islamic Jihad (kill all the non-Moslems) without disclosing that he is a Moslem. <u>This single Moslem, can decimate the whole neighborhood without being caught, especially if he was holding a powerful position</u>.

24. Islamophobia

The web site:
http://crg.berkeley.edu/content/islamophobia/defining-islamophobia
states the following:
The term "Islamophobia" was first introduced as a concept in a 1991 Runnymede Trust Report and defined as "unfounded hostility towards Muslims, and therefore fear or dislike of all or most Muslims." The term was coined in the context of Muslims in the UK in particular and Europe in general, and formulated based on the more common "xenophobia" framework.
The report pointed to prevailing attitudes that incorporate the following beliefs:
•Islam is monolithic and cannot adapt to new realities
•Islam does not share common values with other major faiths
•Islam as a religion is inferior to the West. It is archaic, barbaric, and irrational.
•Islam is a religion of violence and supports terrorism.
•Islam is a violent political ideology.

The key word in this definition is "unfounded". I think after this study of the teachings of Quran and Mohammad, and the **real actions of Moslems around the world**, we should not have any doubt that the hostility towards Moslems is well founded. In addition, all the points describing the attitude of Islam stated above are **well-established facts**.

When people seek their citizen's rights to "**protect themselves and live without fear**", and call for reasonable precautions against Islamic terror (not even to treat Moslems the way Islamic countries treat non-Moslems), **Moslems**, joined by their **Political Prostitutes**, howl loudly objecting to these precautions, and accuse those callers of being racists, Islamophobics, and bigots. However, when news come about the systematic killing, torture, kidnappings, etc. of non-Moslems in Islamic countries, they all disappear and lose their howling voices.

When Donald Trump called for a temporary pause on the coming of Moslems from abroad to the USA until we figure out how to deal with the terrorists that can come within those Moslems, the assumed to be Moderate Moslems inside the USA (because if they were radical Moslems they should not be inside the USA) and all other Moslems around the world, exploded the earth like the hell of a volcano accusing him of being Islamophobic, racist, bigot, etc. They all forgot to raise their voices for many years against Saudi Arabia for not allowing Jews to enter their country, and banning Christians and Jews from practicing their religions, or entering certain cities and areas, knowing that they **never committed any terrorist's act**. They also forgot to criticize Erdogan of Turkey: for supporting terrorists (not only in Syria and Iraq, but also around the world including Europe); for "**killing his own people**" (as Obama keep saying about Assaad); and for invading Iraq and Syria. **THIS SHOWS CLEARLY THE TRUTHFULNESS OF THE DISCUSSIONS IN THIS BOOK, AND HOW MOSLEMS ARE USING OUR TOLERANCE AND FREE SPEECH AGAINST US, TO TERRIFY US, AND SILENCE OUR FREE VOICES**.

When doctors find that, a healthy person has certain kind of cells in his body that can become cancerous cells without alarming signs, the best action that the doctors must take is the **immediate removal of these cells,** even if the removal will impact some of the body functions. Thus, the security agencies in any country must immediately remove any group of people that have the ideology of killing others that are different. The least these agencies must do is the monitoring of those groups.

In fact, Islam's teachings **give Moslems clear methods** to deal with their enemies or **potential enemies** that <u>we should learn and apply</u> "Then, when the sacred months have passed, slay the Moshrekin (infidels) wherever you find them, captivate, besiege, and prepare for them every ambush." [Quran 9:5]. In this statement, Quran is ordering Moslems to do the following to the Moshrekin:

1) **<u>Slay them wherever they are</u>** without delay or waiting for them to commit hostility. Once the conditions to stop these attacks have expired or removed immediately slay them.
2) **<u>Capture them</u>** to disable their ability to cause any harm.
3) **<u>Besiege them</u>** to be able to control and watch them all the time.
4) **<u>Prepare every ambushes for them.</u>**

I found comments on the internet from what seemed to be Moslems approving the ideas that the governments should be suspicious towards Moslems and the citizens of Islamic countries. The governments should monitor them, and take extra precautions against them, which <u>I fully approve as a person from an Islamic country</u>. The **inconvenience for few Moslems** (due to their adoption of the Islamic ideology, and the reach of the Islamic terror to the entire world including Islamic countries), is **<u>completely negligible compared to</u>**:

1) The **trillions of Dollars** wasted on useless securities that **will never stop the terrorist.**
2) The huge **losses of lives** due to Islamic terror.
3) The huge **destructions to properties**.
4) The tremendous **continuous fear** and terror in the **hearts of billions** of people.
5) The huge **losses of time** by billions of travelers around the world.
6) The **invasion of privacy of billions of innocent people,** when traveling or going to places that could be targeted by

Islamic terrorists, because **there is a probability that one out of trillion non-Moslems** could commit a violent act, while there is a **probability that 70 out of 100 Moslems can commit a terrorists' act.**

7) The **inconvenience of billions of innocent people**, when they try to share their fears from Islamic terror, and been **accused of discrimination, Islamophobia, etc**.

8) The **inconvenience of millions** of people to fight the newly invented **unconstitutional laws of "Hate Speech"**, when they call for their governments to take the proper precautions, to **protect them before** Islamic terrorists' actions.

9) The **violation of the constitutional and human rights** of millions of people when they try to speak out and criticize Islam's teachings and terror, and **accusing them of insulting Islam**.

We need laws all over the world, to **protect the citizens from Islamic terror** similar to the **Ku Klux Act** passed by Congress 1871, to **protect US's black citizens** from **Ku Klux Klan's terror**.

Here is a question that needs a **clear honest answer**:

Should we allow a group to open its center in a black community, knowing that this group has the ideology of killing and torturing black people (like the KKK), and practiced this killings for long time inside and outside the USA, <u>and knowing that this group has many peaceful members?</u>

25. The Deception Of The Grand Imam Of Al-Azhar

Sheikh Ahmed Eltayeb, the Grand Imam of Alazhar (the oldest authority in Islamic teachings in the world), addressed the German Parliament on March 16, 2016, trying to draw a good picture of Islam in the western countries. At the **first glance**, the listener will think that what **he said was true**, but <u>it was exactly the deception I explained in this book</u>. I think that the German Parliament was complicit in this deception trying to deceive the people of Germany and the world. Although Germany is the stronghold of Hamed Abdel Samad (the Islamic scholar critical of Islam), no one invited him to explain the facts and show the truth about Islam. They allowed Eltayeb to display small part of the truth, go on without any challenge, and without answering real questions, which I said before is dangerous deception. I am amazed that although Eltayeb knew all these facts and studied them long ago in Elazhar and they are still in its current books, he had the courage to distort the facts. I am glad that Eltayeb had this opportunity, which made his statements spread very quickly all over the media, and no one can retract or hide them.

I respect Eltayeb as one of the most peaceful Islamic scholars in the Islamic establishment. I am not going to attack him personally, but show the real teachings of Islam as one of the respected peaceful scholars tries to show. The readers can find for themselves, if these represent the most peaceful teachings, how the other not so peaceful teachings will be.

1) Eltayeb stated that **Moslems must believe in Christianity and Judaism to be Moslems.** He did not tell us the kind of Jews or Christians that Islam accepts. **<u>Are those the ones that Islam insults, criminalizes, asks Moslems to reject them, and calls them infidels that must be killed??!!</u>** I previously showed that Islam was peaceful at the beginning, when the Prophet Mohammad did not have the power to force his religion, and tried to attract Christians and Jewish people to Islam. However, after Mohammad and his followers migrated from Mecca and

built enough power, the Quran described Christians and Jews in a way to make them disbelievers that must be eliminated "They indeed are disbelievers who say that Jesus the son of Mary is Allah - -"[Quran 5:17]; "They indeed are disbelievers who say that Allah is the Messiah the son of Mary - -"[Quran 5:72]; "They indeed are disbelievers who say that Allah is a Third of Three"[Quran 5:73]. Quran did not like the way Christians and Jewish people describe their relation with God as His children "**Jews and Christians say that we are the children of Allah** and His beloved people - - "[Quran 5:18]. **Finally, Quran did not accept any religion other than Islam** "And **whoever chooses a religion other than Islam, it will not be accepted from him**, and he will be a loser in the Hereafter." [Quran 3:85]. Since this rejection of all other religions came after the peaceful teachings, it is considered an **improvement to the Quran** "Whatever versus We abrogate or cause to be forgotten, We bring (in place) one better than or like it." [Quran 2:106]

2) Eltayeb made bold statements that Islam does not permit the killing of non-Moslems to force them into Islam, or any unjust reason. No need to repeat what I said before that disputes his statements. However, let me remind him of:

   a) **Jihad;** is **killing all non-Moslems to force them into Islam** (until the entire world becomes Islamic), **looting their properties, and enslaving their women and children**.

   b) The Islamic wars against the converts that resulted in the killing of thousands of the converts and forcing the survivors to become Moslems again.

   c) The Deyas (monetary compensation) for killing non-Moslems are fractions of that for a Moslem, and is nothing for atheists or idolaters, which is an explicit invitation to kill them.

3) As for the punishment for converts from Islam, Eltayeb stated :

   a) Islam does not kill converts except when they endanger the society. Again, I do not need to repeat what I said about this issue in the chapter "Converts From Islam Must Be Killed Or Forced To Become Moslems Again". However, the exception of "endangering the society" as a condition to kill the convert, is widely defined in Islam and can include almost anything.

b) He said that **they found** statements by Mohammad (hadith) that set the death penalty for converts. He did not tell us who are those that found them and avoided to state their findings. He was trying to give us the impression that he did not know about them, while every one knows that they are all mentioned in all Sharia books that are studied all over the world in Islamic schools and represent a large part of their text.

c) He contradicted himself, and said that the death penalty for converts is not applied, which is admitting that it exists, but tried to give a peaceful picture of Islam, which has a terrifying teachings.

d) He was misleading the people by saying that; "many men converted and nothing happened to them", instead of saying that; "all converts nothing happened to them". In both cases, the world knows about the converts that were killed, harassed, tortured, and arrested for no reason, the death threats to them, and the "Fatwa" to kill them. Specifically, he knows about the tens of the Egyptian Christians that their religion was recorded by error as Moslems in their official IDs, but the **courts and the authorities** refused to correct their religion to **force them to be Moslems** or face the death penalty for converts.

4) He stated that the word "sward" is not in the Quran once, but hide that the orders to "kill" is mentioned many many times.

5) He stated that there **is freedom of religion in Islam**, which is a **very sad joke**. I do not need to comment on it, but let me remind him of the 3 children (ages under 14) that were sentenced to 3 years in prison each, plus huge financial penalty, after few seconds of a trial in front of an Islamic kangaroo judge, for producing a short video clip mocking ISIS, which the government considered it insulting to Islam. The kangaroo Judge ordered their immediate imprisonment without allowing them to post a bond against the rules, and without waiting for the order to be final. The **Egyptian military president** Elsisi did not care about them, in spite of pretending to be a moderate Moslem (he has the power to cancel the order).

6) He mentioned another sad joke that many atheists are allowed to appear on TV stations. He forgot to tell us the names of those TV stations. Knowing that the Egyptian Moderate Islamic Country, does not allow private TV stations, not to mention the dangers to some one declaring that he is an atheist. This

reminded me of the freedom given to a child (of Moslem father and Christian Mother) when he grows up and have to <u>choose between Islam and Christianity, but he **must choose** the best religion, which is **Islam**, or **death**!! What a freedom!</u>

7) Eltayeb showed clearly the deep mentality of Islam when he explained the reasons Islam does not allow a Moslem woman to marry a non-Moslem man, while a Moslem man can marry any woman (if she was not Christian or Jewish he must force her to become Moslem). He explained it in a deceptive way, saying that Islam accepts Christianity and Judaism as heavenly religions; while they do not accept Islam as a heavenly religion (I showed the deceptive nature of this statement before because **Islam does not accept any other religion**). He added that a Moslem husband would allow his Christian wife to practice her religion freely, while a Christian husband would not allow his Moslem wife to practice Islam freely. He ignored that in all civilized countries the freedom of religion is guaranteed by their constitutions, and **no one can dare to infringe on this freedom for his wife or anyone**. Most importantly the "Freedom of Religion" in these countries are protected and fully enforced, while in Islam it does not exist. **Eltayeb hide the Islamic rule that forces the children of Moslem men to be Moslems** (or get killed).

8) Eltayeb **stated in Germany that the Islamic terrorists do not represent Islam**, while in his speeches **in Egypt, he REFUSED to DECLARE that these TERRORISTS are not Moslems**. This brings us back again to the statement:

<u>NEVER RELY ONLY ON WHAT MOSLEMS SAY OR TEACH OUTSIDE ISLAMIC COUNTRIES.</u> <u>EXAMINE CAREFULLY THE REAL APPLICATIONS OF ISLAM INSIDE THE ISLAMIC SOCIETIES.</u>

26.   The Amazing Swift Proof By Moslems To The Deception Of The Grand Imam Of Al-Azhar

Before the Grand Imam of Alazhar was telling Pope Francis on Monday, **May 24, 2016: "All these are qualities that we share**"; in his country Egypt, and on May 20, 2016, a mob of more than **300 Moslems** prepared for him the proof of his deception, but he ignored it, hoping that no one will know and did his deception anyway.
http://www.independent.co.uk/news/world/africa/elderly-christian-woman-stripped-naked-and-paraded-through-streets-by-mob-a7049926.html
http://www.telegraph.co.uk/news/2016/05/26/hundreds-of-egyptian-muslims-attack-christian-woman-and-homes-af/

The incident happened in the village of Al-Karm (in Minya, Egypt) where **continuous violence against Christians is the norm**. A Moslem man "Nazir Ahmad" wanted to divorce his wife at her fault, so he spread **rumors** that **she loves a Christian man** "Ashraf Abdo Atya". The majority of the Moslems of the village were extremely upset, and without any verifications **wanted to kill Ashraf**, so he was **forced to leave** the village. Nazir's wife filed a complaint with the police and sued her husband "Nazir" claiming that he is defaming and threatening her. She vehemently denied any relationship with Ashraf. On May 19, 2016, Ashraf's parents filed a police report in the main police station of Abo Korkas about threats that will be executed the next day May 20, 2016 (notice that it is Friday, the day of Moslems' prayers). The police ignored it completely and did not take any measures in anticipation of the attacks. Around 8:00 pm (after the Islamic prayers), on May 20, 2016, a mob of about 300 Moslems armed with different weapons; attacked, looted, destroyed, and set fire to 7 Christian's homes just because they are Christians. The mob severely beaten Ashraf's parents, dragged his mother "Soaad Thabet" (70 yrs) to the streets, stripped her completely naked while she was crying and weeping, and paraded her through the village while insulting her. After 2 hours (after 10:00 pm) and after the mob disbursed the police came and arrested 6 men (the media concealed that the arrested were 5 Christians and only 1 Moslem, which was stated on the social media). At least this shows the carelessness of the Egyptian low enforcement to arrest only 6 out of 300. Soaad filed a police report of the crime against her and named the perpetrators as Nazir Ahmad, his brother Abdel Monaam, his father Isaak Ahmed, and others. As usual, the local governor in Minya, General Tarek Nasser, denied that the elderly woman was stripped naked, and said that some irrational youths **threw flammable** missiles at the houses of Christians in the village and some women ran away in their nightgowns. He added that the matter is a minor incident that was resolved, and asked the media to play it down. In his statements, he showed the **extent of his lies**, and his carelessness that committing the criminal actions of **setting fires to homes** (especially **Christian** homes) is a **minor** and **usual** thing that does not require any precautionary actions. A Christian man "Fadl Saad" claimed that the incident was orchestrated by the government, because the police searched the homes of the Christian victims on May 9, 2016, to make sure that they do not have weapons to protect themselves. He stated that the attackers were armed with machine guns, shot guns, heavy sticks, and Molotov bombs. The attackers divided themselves into groups, each assigned to certain task.

If something like this happens to a Moslem woman just once (not going on for tens of years) in a non-Islamic country, the Governor, Police Chief, the police officers in the police station, and every one that did not do the actions required to prevent such incident, will be swiftly arrested, prosecuted, and the president may **resign**. Additionally, Moslems of all kinds, around the world will erupt into violent demonstrations that might include the killings of innocent Christians, and they may demand the UN to issue rules to protect Islam. However, because the Egyptian president El-Sisi is a follower of the religion of peace, he promised that the military will repair the burned homes, and ordered the authorities to investigate the incident (before his direct order, no one cared to do anything and every one was lying to hide the truth, and they are still lying). Notice that in the last few years in Egypt, Moslems; burned about **100 churches**, kidnapped more than **500 underage** girls, looted and burned tens of Christian homes, and killed, injured, and falsely prosecuted and imprisoned tens of Christians; without any compensation to the victims and very few Moslems were arrested.

We should note the following:

1) In light of the previous story, we can tell that **Islam shares some values with Christianity in <u>words only as needed</u>, but has its own values as demonstrated by the actions of those 300 Moslem mobs, and the actions and inactions of the Egyptian Moslem authorities**.

2) Assuming that those 300 Moslem men are radical terrorists and the rest of the village are different grades of Moslems, and assuming that less than 10% of a group will participate in criminal actions like this, we can estimate that the total number of Moslem terrorists in this village is more than 3000. If we assume that each one of the 300 is a member of a family of 4, then the total number will be more than 12,000. The population of this village is about 20,000; about 15% to 30% are Christians, we can estimate the total Moslem population is about 16,000. Then there are about 20% (3000/16000) to 75% (12000/16000) Moslem terrorists in this Moslem population. **<u>This is close to my estimate that 30% of Moslems are radicals (terrorists) and more than 75% are potential terrorists.</u>**

3) In such cases, the <u>police always arrest at least **one known criminal** that has nothing to do with the incident (to divert public attention and put the blame on him), **most of the Christian victims, one or two actual Moslem perpetrators**, and **few innocent Moslems** to **make up a number**</u>. <u>Later the prosecutor may find that most of the Moslems arrested were innocent (which could be true), and the known criminal(s) either accept the blame for a hidden compensation or the court clears them.</u> **Then all the blame and punishments will be on the Christian victims**.

4) Those kinds of attacks are the normal daily life for Christians in Egypt since Sadaat became a president, and many times the authorities orchestrate such attacks.

5) This incident exposed the **deception** about the marriage of Moslems to non-Moslems. In this case, **extreme violence** irrupted just for rumors that a **Moslem woman** is in love with a **Christian man**.

6) Extreme violence and humiliation against women is part of Islam as demonstrated by the prophet Mohammad when he ordered the **killing of Om Kerfa and Asmaa Bent-Marawan**.

7) The promise of president El-Sisi to repair the burned homes by the military has its advantages and disadvantages. The only advantage is that the fixing could be faster than the government but the owners are much faster. Some of the disadvantages are:
   a) The military is distracted and overwhelmed by minor civil activities.
   b) The victims have to wait for the military to do the repairs, putting them under pressure to surrender many of their rights.
   c) The victims will lose their rights for fair compensations, which should be many times the actual damages.
   d) Will encourage, and already encouraged, the continuation of more violence against Christians.
   e) It will be an excuse to close the criminal case against the perpetrators, bury the facts of the case, hide the terrorists, and thwart the taking of any precautions to prevent such incidents in the future.
   f) It will hide the responsibilities of the authorities and the whole government.

Up until now, El Sisi did not fulfill his promises, and the burned churches are still waiting. Additionally, more violent incidents like the one in El Karm happened in El Aamerya (a village west of Alexandria), and another village in the middle of Nile-Delta.

CHAPTER THREE

OBAMA'S ACTIONS AND INACTIONS

Obama declared ISIS to be a terrorist organization and said; "So ISIL speaks for no religion. Their victims are overwhelmingly Muslim, and no faith teaches people to massacre innocents. No just God would stand for what they did yesterday, and for what they do every single day." Obama is wrong in the first, second, and third sentences. He knew well that the name ISIS tells him clearly their religion, knew that their victims are overwhelmingly non-Moslems (not Moslems as he is misrepresenting), and knew that Christianity is not the one that teaches people to massacre innocent or even guilty people. However, he is correct when he said; "No just God would stand for what they did yesterday and for what they do every single day". Obama was <u>truthful</u> when he said; "ISIL is a **terrorist organization, pure and simple. And it has no vision other than the slaughter of all who STAND in its way**." Although he did not add clarification to this statement, it is well understood now that he was describing two things that are **one thing, which is very pure and very simple, but many people try to deceive themselves and others and separate it into two things**. However, I would like to add a note that the **Christians** of: Iraq, Syria, Egypt, and other countries, are **peaceful** people that **never stood in ISIL's way**.

These statements and many other statements by Obama and his administration, policies, actions, and inactions, need books to explain them not just a book like this. In the following we will examine some of Obama's statements, actions, and inactions.

126

1. Is Obama A Muslim?

One of the great things about this Great Nation is that no one is discriminated against for his religion, color, origin, etc. The anti-discrimination laws are not just written statements, but actual laws with the mechanisms to guarantee their fair applications. The best proof for this was the election of Obama as a president. **At the beginning, not every one paid attention to his religion or questioned it because it could be illegal, and people were interested in what he would do to his country not what he would do to his religion**. But after Obama's questionable actions, inactions, and statements, which showed that he is promoting and defending Islam on the expense of the USA (I could not say "on the expense of his country the USA", because Obama might not take the USA as his country, and according to the teachings of Islam, **Islam itself is a religion and a country**). The question of his religion became very important because he is now violating the US laws and its Constitution by promoting Islam while discriminating against the non-Muslims.

Obama's birth certificate has a lot of doubt about its validity. But what is not disputed is that his father was a Muslim and he spent the early part of his life in Islamic country (Indonesia) where he attended an Islamic school (Madrassa). According to the teachings of Islam, because Obama's father was a Muslim Obama has no choice except to be a Muslim or he would be killed. This rule is enforced in all Islamic countries including Indonesia. The Islamic schools (Madrassa) are designed to teach and brain wash the young kids to be devoted Muslims and apply all the teachings of Islam including Jihad and Taqyia. Hence, we can say that Obama is officially a Muslim (if he was to obtain official documents that displays his religion – as is the case in most Islamic countries - then it will show his religion as Islam). On the same time, he could be a **Taqyia Muslim** denying that his religion is Islam to **benefit Islam or harm the non-Muslims**. It is obvious that when Obama denies that he is a Muslim, he can defend and benefit Islam better than stating his religion is Islam.

2. The Misrepresentation That The Majority Of ISIS's Victims Are Muslims

Obama stated that ISIL's "victims are overwhelmingly Muslim", which is misleading. ISIS (and Sunni Islam) consider that Shiite Moslems are more dangerous to Islam than Christians and Jews. From ISIS's point of view, all the non-Sunni Moslems are not Moslems, and <u>everyone that opposes them, are all enemies of Islam that must be killed</u>. More importantly, the purpose of this statement is to justify not taking any reasonable action against ISIS for their atrocities committed against Christians. Obama (**being biased against Christianity**) was trying to show that he is not biased against Christians, because he also did not care about the killings of Moslems. Obama contradicted himself when he said that ISIL is not Islamic and its victims are Muslims. Obama is setting himself to be the one that can determine if someone is a Muslim or not. He ignores that according to Islamic teachings, it is good enough for any one to say: "No Allah but One Allah, and Mohammad is the prophet of Allah", to become immediately a Muslim (irrespective of his deeds as explained before). In addition, if that Moslem changes his religion later, he must be killed. **Obama is amazing in his misrepresentation when he admits that ISIL "selectively apply certain versus of the Quran"**. How and why he considered that when someone selectively applies certain rules from a set of rules that he is not following this set of rules. <u>Obama has a legal background and knows well that this is exactly what lawyers do.</u> **<u>If there is any conflict between two or more individual rules in any set of rules, this invalidates the whole set not guilt the one who selectively apply the rules</u>**. Obama knows the facts that ISIL declared themselves as Muslims, raising the Islamic flag, apply versus of the Quran, and following the teachings of Islam, but he denies the truth that they are Muslims, and did not provide any proof from the Islamic teachings to prove that they are not Muslims.

3. Obama's Preparation To Convert The USA To An Islamic Country

Obama enriched his administration and the top positions in the government with Muslims, in preparation to promote Islam instead of protecting the US constitution, its citizens, interests, and human rights. Here are some examples of those positions.

- John Brennan, current head of the CIA converted to Islam while stationed in Saudi Arabia.
- Obama's top Advisor, Valerie Jarrett, is a Muslim who was born in Iran where her parents still live.
- Hillary Clinton's top advisor, Huma Abedin is a Muslim, whose mother and brother are involved in the now Outlawed "Muslim Brotherhood" in Egypt.
- Assistant Secretary For Policy Development for Homeland Security, Arif Aikhan, is a Muslim.
- Homeland Security Advisor, Mohammed Elibiary, is a Muslim.
- Obama advisor and founder of the Muslim Public Affairs Council, Salam al-Marayati, is a Muslim.
- Obama's Sharia Czar, Imam Mohamed Magid, of the Islamic Society of North America is a Muslim.
- Advisory Council on Faith-Based Neighborhood Partnerships, Eboo Patel, is a Muslim.

A new trend of taking the oath on things other than the Bible is showing now. CIA director John Brennan took his oath on a copy of the Constitution, not a Bible, and Congressman Keith Ellison took his oath on a copy of the Quran. Since these two persons are Moslems, many questions are raised about their faith and what kind of Muslims are they? The teachings of Islam in some parts consider the Bible and the Torah are Holy books like the Holy Quran, hence, a Muslim should have no objection taking oath on the Bible as it is a Holy Book. On the other hand, the teachings of Islam in other parts condemned Christians and Jews, called for the killing of all Jews, and categorized Christians as disbelievers that must be killed. It is obvious from this simple analysis the kind of direction these two Muslims will take in their work.

These appointments and the mentioned new trend explain why Obama and his cronies are systematically destroying our nation, supporting Islamic terrorists groups worldwide, and ignoring the genocide perpetrated on Christians all over Africa and the Middle East.

4. Obama Regards the USA as One of the Biggest Muslim Nations

During an interview on France's Canal+ TV Channel (October 2014), Obama said that the American people need to be better educated about Islam, since US could and should be regarded as a Muslim country. He said that the number of Muslims residing in the US makes it "one of the biggest Muslim nations".
http://www.jerusalemonline.com/news/world-news/around-the-globe/obama-defines-us-as-muslim-country-8785
No need to dispute this irresponsible statement from the president of the USA, because anyone can tell that it is not true. However, it reflects his bias towards whatever is Islamic irrespective of the truth. This statement and many other statements, reflect his policies, and his way of giving misleading information. The only correct part is that the American people (and the entire world including Muslims) need to be better educated about the real full Islam, and this book should be a minimum start.

5. Obama And His Close Ties With Islamic Organizations

Around November 17, 2014, Perry Chiaramonte published an article about CAIR (Council On American Islamic Relations). He said that CAIR enjoys close ties with the Obama administration. It was one of 82 groups around the world designated terrorist

organizations by the United Arab Emirates. While CAIR has previously been linked to Hamas, it has held hundreds of meetings with White House officials on a wide range of community issues and has sought to present itself as a mainstream Muslim organization [http://www.foxnews.com/us/2014/11/17/us-group-cair-added-to-terror-list-by-united-arab-emirates/].
The US constitution prohibits the USA government from having any relations with religious organizations to promote them. I never heard about a Christian, organization for Christian relations.

Although many countries listed the Muslim Brotherhood organization and other Islamic organizations affiliated with it as terrorist's organizations, Obama White House have close ties with them, and continuously having meetings with their members. http://www.breitbart.com/national-security/2015/02/07/the-muslim-brotherhood-comes-to-the-white-house/
Among the Muslim "leaders" who met with Obama were individuals with disturbingly close ties to the global Muslim Brotherhood. Azhar Azeez, President of the Islamic Society of North America (ISNA). ISNA was founded in 1981 by members of the Muslim Brotherhood. The group was listed as an unindicted co-conspirator in the Holy Land Foundation terrorism financing trial. Federal prosecutors have previously described how ISNA funneled its money to "the Palestinian Mujahadeen," the original name for the HAMAS military wing. Azeez is also a founding member of CAIR Dallas/Fort Worth Chapter. In October, 2014, Azeez signed a letter endorsing Sharia Islamic governance. Hoda Elshishtawy of the Muslim Public Affairs Council (MPAC) attended the Muslim leaders' meeting with Obama. Mohamed Majid, who serves as Imam of the All Dulles Area Muslim Society (ADAMS), also attended the White House meeting with the President, and senior advisors Ben Rhodes and Valerie Jarrett. Majid is also an official with the brotherhood-affiliated Islamic Society of North America (ISNA). The Muslim Brotherhood's motto remains: "Allah is our objective. The Prophet is our leader. Quran is our law. **Jihad is our way. Dying in the way of Allah is our highest hope.**"
The son of Khairat al-Shatter (top ranking Brotherhood member), threatened to expose documents that would land Obama in prison. In addition, Morsi's wife threatened to publish letters from Hillary Clinton, exposing "special relationship" between Muslim

Brotherhood and Obama Administration
[http://www.jihadwatch.org/2014/08/morsis-wife-threatens-to-publish-letters-from-hillary-clinton-exposing-special-relationship-between-muslim-brotherhood-and-obama-administration].

Egyptian Official Tahani al-Gebali (Vice President of the Supreme Constitutional Court in Egypt) claimed to have proof and documents that could send Obama to prison. These documents would explain why the Obama administration is so vehemently supportive of the Muslim Brotherhood, whose terrorism, has among other atrocities, caused the destruction of some 80 Christian churches in less than one week
[http://freedomoutpost.com/2013/08/second-source-egyptian-official-tahanial-gebali-claims-to-have-documents-proof-that-could-send-obama-to-prison/].

6. Obama: The New Preacher And Defender Of Islam

Obama stated in his remarks to the UN General Assembly (September 2012): **"The future must not belong to those who slander the prophet of Islam. But to be credible, those who condemn that slander must also condemn the hate we see in the images of Jesus Christ that are desecrated, or churches that are destroyed, or the Holocaust that is denied."**
[http://www.whitehouse.gov/the-press-office/2012/09/25/remarks-president-un-general-assembly]
We can see easily how Obama is trying to involve Christians and Jews and pretend that he is defending them. Obama knows well that Christianity was spreading because of its rightful teachings, not because some one was protecting it against slander, torture, or killing. The denial of Holocaust will not slander Judaism. Mr. Obama, it is not acceptable for some one occupying the position of the President of the USA, to just condemn burning and destroying churches, especially in areas where the USA has control over, caused serious destructions and damages, or caused armed conflicts

that killed hundreds of thousands of innocent people. Mr. Obama, it is your responsibility, not just to condemn by words, it is to **swiftly act to stop** these terrible actions before and after they happen, harshly punish the perpetrators, and compensate their victims for all the destruction and damages they caused.

Now, for the more important statement: "**The future must not belong to those who slander the prophet of Islam**." What is Obama's definition for "slander"?!!! Is slander when some one practices his freedom of expression in a movie showing historical facts? Is slander when some one practices his freedom of religion and criticizes another religion? Obama must understand that he is not responsible about the personal actions of the US citizens, but responsible about defending their constitution rights. **Obama must understand that Islam is a religion that not only ridicule and slander other religions, but also, criminalizes the following of anything other than Islam, and makes death its punishment**.

On September 24, 2014, in his Address to the UN, Obama said; "**We reject any suggestion of a clash of civilizations**." Let us first examine the meaning of "Civilization": It is the development of a human society from a savage, uneducated, or unrefined state to an advanced state, in which a higher level of culture, art, science, industry, and government has been reached. I leave the reader to compare the conditions of societies before and after they became Islamic. This comparison will tell us if there is a clash of civilizations, development of higher civilizations, revival of savage conditions, or anything else.

7. Obama's Support To The Terrorists

Obama and his administration supported the Islamic terrorists all over the world, while pretending that they are fighting them. The best example was when he gave the green light to ISIL to go ahead and kill, loot, destroy, and expand with **his assurance** that he **will not send any troops** that can cause any real threat to ISIL. He declared that he would build a **haphazard coalition** from incapable or unwilling countries to fight ISIL, and use airplanes to bomb them, which could need three years to defeat ISIL. While Obama did not respect the law (he himself participated in drafting) regarding the negotiation with terrorists, he released five Moslem terrorists and sat free one US army deserter (instead of prosecuting him for treason) for nothing. Although Obama has the power to take swift action against ISIL without Congress' approval, he pretended that he would seek its approval. No one needs to be an expert in the USA's politics to **understand the game Obama is playing**, to give ISIS all the time they need to achieve their goals, while the Congress could take a month, a year, a decade, and hopefully not a century to give its approval.

Obama and his administration allowed Alkaeda to open an office in Qatar, and supported the Moslem Brotherhood (they have the same ideology and methods of terror like Alkaeda). Obama encouraged and emboldened the Jihadists by his inactions against their terror everywhere, and not even asking his Moderate Moslems to raise their voices or do something effective against that terror. One of the examples is Iraq. Obama and the world saw clearly the brutal killing of innocent Christians, and the looting and burning of their churches, businesses, and properties, but no effective action was taken by the USA, World, or Obama's Moderate Moslems, for many years. Keeping in mind that the USA is fully responsible about the deteriorating situation in Iraq. A better example is the support that the Moslem Brotherhood in Egypt got from Obama, in spite of their brutalities that was taking place for many years before and after they came to power. Their brutalities were directed to Christians, which included killing, burning churches, looting properties, killing the Christian monks in their monasteries and destroying their precious artifacts and books. Kidnapping Christians and their children is the normal life now in Egypt (more than 600 girls were kidnapped for forced marriage and to convert them to Islam). All these brutalities were happening in front of the eyes of the US government, International Community, and the Egyptian government. The Egyptian government was supporting these brutalities and even punishing harshly the Christian victims when they complain. Obama gave the Moslem Brotherhood millions of Dollars, and supported them politically beyond the reasonable diplomatic protocol. Even when the Egyptian people revolted in millions in a historical way against the Moslem Brotherhood and its president Mohammad Morsie, and an **Egyptian Court in the city of Ismailia issued an arrest warrant against him during his presidency**, Obama still wanted him to come to power against the will of the Egyptian people, and against the Egyptian criminal law. This shows clearly how Obama is supporting the criminals without doing any effective action for their victims.

Obama expressed his rejection to freedom of religion, and condemned the movie that he perceived to be insulting to Islam and himself personally. Further, when the massacre of Charlie Hebdo happened (January 7, 2015), **he refused to attend or send a USA senior representative to the "Stand For Freedom Of Speech Unity March" (January 12, 2015), in which the world stood together in the wake of terrorist Charlie Hebdo attack**. Attorney General Eric Holder was already in Paris, but no one cared upon sending him. **Obama's inaction** sent a clear message to the world that **he sympathizes with the terrorists, and supports them**. As a result, a huge demonstration of British Muslims gathered in London to protest against Muhammad cartoons (February 8, 2015), and provided a petition signed by more than 100,000 British Muslims. It called for "global civility" and says the production of cartoons of Mohammad are "an affront to the norms of civilized society". [http://www.theguardian.com/world/2015/feb/08/british-muslims-london-protest-against-muhammad-cartoon-charlie-hebdo] I hoped to hear the hundreds of thousands of Moslems around the world show their condemnation of Islamic terror, if they actually consider it terror, when thousands of non-Moslems were massacred on the hands of Moslems. The world needs to know their definition of "global civility" and "civilized society", which I am going to discuss in more detail shortly.

8. Obama's Disrespect And Rejection To The International Human Standards And Adoption of Islamic Terror Standards

In my previous discussions in this book, I showed that Obama is continuously and consistently disrespecting the US constitution, the International Human rights, and the Civilized Human Standards, while adopting the Islamic Terror Standards. On "National Day of Prayer" (February 5th, 2015) Obama said, "Just because you have the right to say something doesn't mean the rest of us shouldn't question those who would insult others in the name of free speech." Obama used many times words like "insult" and "slander" to describe his opinion about the people that use their freedom of speech to express their opinions about Islam. The main question is: Who define these words? And how? Obama focuses on insults to Islam and slander to the prophet Mohammad, irrespective of the facts. I am going to give very few examples related to these issues:

1. Quran and Mohammad describe repeatedly the non-Moslems as infidels that should be killed and humiliated. Moslems strongly believe that these are Allah's orders, while all non-Moslems consider them **not only insults, but also assaults, invitation and provocation of criminal actions**.
2. Quran talks about **Saint Mary** stating; **"Your father was not a wicked man nor was your mother a prostitute"**. [Quran 19:28]. Christians consider this a **vulgar insulting statement** that should have been stated more appropriately as "Your father was an **honorable man** and your mother an **honorable woman**", which is also a **better linguistic expression**. Moslems believe that all the text of the Quran is a miraculous linguistic text that no human, angle, or genie can write anything like it or improve it, and **Allah is praising St. Mary with this language!!**
3. Quran talks about **Saint Mary** stating; "And Mary - - who **guarded her vagina**." [Quran 66:12]. Again, Christians consider this a **vulgar insulting statement** that should have been stated more appropriately as "And Mary - - who guarded her purity.", which is better linguistic expression. Again,

Moslems believe that Allah is praising St. Mary with this language!

Hopefully, after these few examples, Obama and the angry Moslems, be more careful before saying that someone is slandering The prophet Mohammad or insulting Islam.

9. The Innocence Of Obama

Obama came after the beheading of Jim Foley and Steven Sotloff, pretending to be innocent, as if he just new about the beheading of these two men without any knowledge of the hundreds that were beheaded during his six years of presidency, and the many years before it. He just returned from playing golf, or wake up from his deep peaceful sleep, during which he forgot his calls to enforce human rights and spreading democracy, and **forgot to do anything to stop the slaughter of all those innocent people**.

10. Who Can Fight ISIS?

Obama is building coalition to fight ISIS, formed from Moderate Islamic countries. I just explained the fiction of Moderate in Islam. There are also many obvious reasons that Islamic countries would not fight ISIS effectively. One of them is that Islam strictly prohibits Moslems from fighting or killing of another Moslem. However, killing Moslems to Moslems could be justified easily, by claiming that those Moslems are converts, enemies of Islam, harming Islam, or hiding their bad intentions towards Islam under Taqyiah principle. Although Islamic teachings could be interpreted easily to do thing or its opposite by hiding the unwanted ones, **when it comes to Moslems killing Moslems, Moslems prefer to kill the non-Moslems instead**. This tells us that they might start by fighting ISIS within their own limitations until they achieve their own goals, and then turn themselves against the USA (study the history of the USA in Afghanistan). However, let us examine the possibility of this coalition based on the benefits each country can get from fighting ISIS.

1. Turkey

Turkey is a country that supports ISIS, and allows a large number of foreign Jihadists to cross its borders to join jihad. A huge number of Turkey's population do not consider ISIS a terrorist group, and has the same goal of building an Islamic Khalafi-state. Turkey has the intention to eliminate the Kurdish population from inside and outside and hoping that ISIS can finish this job quickly for them without any effort or blame from the international community. I expect that Turkey will pretend to fight ISIS but do the opposite on the ground (Taqyia), until they achieve their own goals, then withdraw.

2. Saudi Arabia

Saudi Arabia is a country that applies the Islamic Teachings in a way to suppress its people, and keep the resources (mainly oil), and the power in the hands of the Saudi family. Saudi Arabia is one of the countries that heavily supported ISIS and its ideology. However, ISIS now is using the same weapon, Islamic Teachings, to present to the Saudis an Islamic state more Islamic than what is now in the Kingdom. This means that ISIS will eventually replace the Saudi family in their positions. I expect that Saudi Arabia will participate in a limited fight against ISIS until they feel safe then withdraw.

3. Egypt

Egypt is an Islamic country, and its president is a devoted Moslem that is unwilling or unable to fight or control the Islamists in Egypt, in spite of declaring them to be a terrorist organization. It has a large useless army that controls about 40% of its economy and is unable to stop terrorists' activities around the borders of Egypt or inside the country itself. Egypt, like any other Islamic country, has a large number of people that supports ISIS and do not consider it as a terrorist group. Its president would not risk the revolt of Islamists against him. Hence, Egypt will not support the fight against ISIS.

4. Iraq

After the USA invaded Iraq under the cover "establish democracy", it did the opposite when Iraq enacted its constitution that made "Sharia" the main source of legislation. This established a religious country with no rights for non-Moslems, and started a brutal war between the "Sunni Moslems" and the "Shiite Moslems". Now if the USA supported the Shiite to fight and defeat ISIS, what is the point at which we can say we succeeded? Is it the elimination of Sunni, which is impossible? Moreover, even after defeating ISIS there is no guarantee that the Shiite will not turn against the USA.

5. Iran

Iran is an Islamic state that has a Shiite majority. Well known for violating human rights, and the USA still have a problem with its nuclear program.

6. Syria

The USA helped ISIS in Syria, and did not take any action to stop the brutality of its fighters for many years, especially at the beginning when it was easy to defeat them. The whole world saw pictures and videos beyond any imagination, and the International Community did not do anything, because Obama wanted to kill one person, its president (dictator). **Obama allowed and supported, the slaughter of hundreds of thousands of innocent Syrians, and the destruction of their economy and society, for many years**. The Syrian army and the Kurdish are the only forces that could challenge ISIS. The USA needs to revise its policies first towards these two possible candidates.

11. The Disaster Of Benghazi

The attack on the American Embassy in Benghazi (Libya) and the killing of the American citizens was not an isolated incident. It was the result of the Obama's policy to cooperate with and support the Islamic Jihadists. I believe that **Obama and Hillary Clinton, with the help of the many Moslems** that came to the White House after he was elected, negotiated and made secret agreements with the Jihadists. Jihadists would not attack the American targets, so that Obama can say that during his presidency he kept the USA safe, in return, the USA will support the Jihadists in other parts of the world. When the news and warnings came with the dangerous situation around the USA Embassy, Obama and Hillary ignored them completely, they thought that their secret agreements would prevent any disaster. However, Obama and Hillary fell deeply into the Taqyiah, and the complete disaster happened. Another disaster happened after Benghazi's Disater, which was hiding and denying it, and Hillary made her famous statement that; **"it does not matter now"**. Adding insults to injury, both Obama and Hillary, apologized publicly to the Moslems, about the film that showed historical true-facts that are well documented in the Islamic sources, **INSTEAD of asking at least those "Moderate Moslems" to apologize for the barbaric actions of the other Moslems**. From my point of view, **THIS APOLOGY IS A CRIME AGAINST ALL THE US CITIZENS AND THE US CONSTITUTION**. Instead of this apology, they should have expressed their support and protection for this person. This apology is a crime against this US citizen that made the film, and practiced his constitutional rights to express his opinion. **It is an explicit justification and approval of the barbaric actions of the Jihadists**, and any future barbaric actions, that would endanger the safety of this citizen and all other persons who try to practice their basic human rights and express their opinion, without fearing for: their lives, safety, family's lives, family's safety, and properties. Obama and Hillary have good knowledge of the law, should have knowledge of the USA constitution, and **must know their duties to respect and protect the USA's constitution and citizens**. Hence, both Obama and Hillary, **should be prosecuted** for the Benghazi disaster, and what followed it from concealments, and **apologies**.

12. Bergdahl

Let me remind you of Sergeant Bowe Bergdahl that spent about five years with the Taliban in Afghanistan, who was traded illegally by President Obama for five top Taliban commanders who were in U.S. custody (May 31, 2014). Soldiers in Bergdahl's unit accused him of deserting. Up until now, the results of the Army's investigations were not released (supposed to be completed by August 15, 2014). This is beyond the dreams of the terrorists to have this number of them released, for such a low price of one soldier. If the accusations that he deserted his unit are true (I believe to be true), it will make it impossible for Obama to deny that he really supports the Islamic terrorists to his maximum ability. Let us wait and see if something will be concealed like the Benghazi incident.

13. Osama Bin Laden

The way the Obama administration handled the story of capturing and killing Bin Laden is worth examining. I understand and confident, that the USA's army have resources and military expertise not available to many countries and beyond my imagination. Nevertheless, for me as a normal person without military experience, I would arrange an operation to capture Bin Laden alive with maximum information (computers, documents, etc). I think this is a logical goal that the administration would share with me. Simply, because if the goal was just to kill him, one or more guided missiles could have done it easily, as the USA used to do. The next step is to prepare highly skilled team of army fighters to go and physically attack and capture him. To capture him alive, I will need a tool to disable him (make him unconscious and unable to resist). Which could be rubber pullets filled with: tranquilizer, pigmentation (to simulate blood), and material to stop heavy bleeding. These pullets could be propelled by a special silenced guns and reduced explosive charge, to give the required impact and damage at short distance, without going deep under the skin or clothes causing death. The members of the team should have good protective bullet-proof vests, and accompanied by a paramedic with the proper preparation to keep him alive in case of life threatening injury. As for the surprise element that could fail due to the noise of the helicopter, I would let the helicopter bass many days very close to the target location until the target people think it is a routine flight every day at the same time, and they are not alarmed any more when they hear it coming or going. I think that this is exactly what the Navy SEALs did, and further <u>succeeded in capturing Bin Laden alive</u> (against Obama's claims that he was killed).

Many factors ascertain that Bin Laden was captured alive:

4. More than three different conflicting stories describing his death, number of shots, places of shots-injuries, his resistance or not, his reactions, and his wife's reactions. The truth has one consistent story only.

5. One of the stories about how Bin Laden was killed described two shots to the front of his head that made him fall shaking, and a third shot to his chest killed him. No one described the result of these shots. The first thing **if these shots were normal shots fired at these very short distances, they must penetrate his scull or body and <u>come out from the other side, which did not happen</u>, indicating that they were not regular shots.** The second thing, a regular bullet hitting the brain will cause immediate death without shaking, and without a need for additional shot to his chest. We can correct this story and say that the two shots to his head were made from very soft material to cause very strong hit to his head causing him to become unconscious for few seconds without causing death (as if hit with a heavy stick to his head). The third shot to his chest had the tranquilizing material to keep him sedated for some time.

6. The time line of the actions does not match the practical situation, and the amount of time from the start of the operation until the burial is impossible (about 7 hours). Moreover, there is no justification to expedite any of the steps after killing him (it does not make any difference for a dead body), except if they want to hide the truth. The distance between Abbottabad in Pakistan and the USA base in Afghanistan is about 440 Km, which needs about 1.5 hours to travel with a helicopter flying at 300 Km/Hr. The direct distance between the USA base in Afghanistan and the North of the Arabian Golf is about 2000 Km (difficult to reach range for a helicopter), going above

dangerous places (inside Iran) with a precious cargo. Therefore, it is logical to avoid this direct route, which can make the distance exceed the 3000 Km of about 10 hours flight, which could be beyond the ability of a helicopter.

7. It does not make sense to risk this precious cargo (or dead body), go, and bury it in the Arabian Golf, with the <u>joke of executing an</u> **<u>Islamic burial</u>**. Since when the USA cared about Islamic burial **<u>except Obama</u>**?! I do not know if any one on this USA ship knows what an Islamic burial is, may be they have some Taqyiah Moslems on board?!!! What exactly was done during this Islamic burial?! (I am not sure if the burial could be described as Islamic, ISIS-Fashion, barbaric, civilized, etc.) This does not convince me, but it might convince Obama and his administration. If he was really killed, and they wanted to bury him, it could have been done very easily and very cheep in the air above the mountains (closer to hell and heaven), with enough explosive charge.

My conclusion is that Bin Laden was captured alive and stayed alive for some time.

CHAPTER FOUR

COMMENTS ON THE NEWS

1. Comments on Benghazi Report Released November 21, 2014
(November 25, 2014)

The "Executive Summary" of the "Benghazi Report" Released November 21, 2014, by the House Permanent Select Committee on Intelligence ("HPSCI"), said that it: "focused on the activities of the Intelligence Community ("IC") before, during, and after the attacks." No one needs to read such report and waste time on it to find out if IC was negligent or not. From the beginning, after the preliminary hearings, it was clear that the blame goes directly to Obama, Hillary, and Obama's Administration. They were negligent in dealing with the Benghazi's issue. For this Committee to waste all these resources, waste all this time, and delay the findings is unacceptable. For me, this report and its findings are just another sad joke like the Islamic burial of Bin Laden, and naked trial to divert the attention and the responsibilities away from the real issues and the perpetrators (burial of the truth).

2. Comments on Obama's Prediction of Defeating ISIS within Three Years
(December 20, 2014)

U.S. Secretary of State John Kerry said, "We're convinced that in the days ahead we have the ability to destroy ISIL,- - - It may take a year, it may take two years, it may take three years. But we're determined it has to happen." [http://www.businessinsider.com/john-kerry-isis-obama-destroy-coalition-2014-9]

Why is the rush?!!! What a determination to make it happen?!!! We can wait until ISIS kills and slaughters all the non-Moslems, change the whole region beyond repair, while Obama is just condemning those atrocities with just his mouth. **It does not matter for Obama the lives of non-Moslems, he is happy playing golf, why bother**. Just a reminder, that the USA led a military operation (Desert Storm) to liberate Kuwait from Iraqi forces (well armed and organized force) in few days not few years as Obama is projecting to defeat ISIS (gang or terrorists).

There are many theories that the US does not want to stop the Islamic state (ISIL) – only exploit them for other means. [Steve Chovanec (Global Research, November 16, 2014), http://www.globalresearch.ca/the-us-doesnt-want-to-stop-the-islamic-state-isil-only-exploit-them-for-other-means/5414354]

3. Comments on the "Pakistani-Americans March Downtown To Protest Taliban Attack On School"
(December 28, 2014)

There were about 12 persons from the Chicago's Pakistani-American community on December 27, 2014, came out to the Chicago-Loop Saturday to protest the Taliban's attack on a school in Pakistan on December 16, 2014. It is good for peaceful Moslems to condemn the Islamic terror against Moslems, but it could have been better if they **had condemned also the slaughter of thousands of non-Moslems**. On the same time, comparing this negligible number of 12 to the 100,000 that signed a petition against The prophet Mohammad's cartoons, and to the millions that demonstrated violently against the things they perceived as distasteful to Islam, give us a clear idea about the ratio of peaceful active Moslems (moderate Moslems) to other Moslems. Even when this tiny percent (of moderate Moslems) demonstrate against the violence, they condemn the violence against Moslems only, and condole the non-Moslems by saying the meaningless words that "Islam is a religion of peace".

4. Comments on the "Indiana's Freedom Of Religion Law"

Any law that allows people to act towards others according their religious believes only is wrong. Imagine what can happen if a Moslem that abides with the teachings of Islam that calls for the killings of all non-Moslems and looting their properties, is running his business according to his religious believes?!!!!   Religions should always be separated from the laws and government. People are free to enact their laws guided by the religious believes of the majority, so long as these laws do not infringe on the rights, freedom, wellbeing of others, or violate the constitution. Please, do not ignore the lessons from ISIS, and the Islamic Sharia Laws.

5. Comments on the "Scandals of Hillary Clinton"

It is well known that Hillary Clinton was a lawyer and knows very well the laws and the penalties for violating them. She was using her personal server to run the business of the Office of the Secretary of State (email). For me, it means that she was running the office as her own business for her own benefits. When her actions were disclosed to the public, **she played the innocence of a 5 years old child and said that those actions were not good ideas, instead of calling them with their real legal terms under the criminal law**. She went further in her illegal actions and removed the emails that she pretended to be personal, with her full knowledge that mixing business communications with personal ones removes any personal privilege from all of them.

6. Comments on the finding that "Bergdahl Deserted His Unit"

Finally, after trials to hide the truth and unnecessary delays, the disastrous fact that Bergdahl deserted his army unit was proved as everyone expected. Another disastrous situation to eliminate the just punishment is playing now. Instead of having the "Commander **In-Cheat**" and the "Deserter" **<u>prosecuted</u>**, we hear repeated voices saying, "What difference does it make".

7. Comments on the "Hillary's Additional Lies And Scandals"

Now, after honest people - not the Congress - showed that the LAWYER Hillary Clinton is LYING, she changed her tactic to attack the HONEST people under her well known principles "it does not matter" and "what difference it make". I strongly believe that Naglaa Ali Mahmoud (the wife of the former Moslem Brotherhood president of Egypt Morsie) was truthful when she claimed that she had a business relationship with Hillary and have documents that should send Hillary to PRISON.
http://elw3yalarabi.org/modules.php?name=News&file=article&sid=15312

8. Comments on Seymour Hersh's finding that "Obama's Story About Bin Ladin is a Lie"

The investigative journalist Seymour Hersh found that Obama's story about killing Bin Laden is a lie.
http://www.vox.com/2015/5/11/8584473/seymour-hersh-osama-bin-laden
Hersh said that Pakistani intelligence services captured bin Laden in 2006 and kept him locked up with support from Saudi Arabia, using him as leverage against al-Qaeda. In 2010, Pakistan agreed to sell bin Laden to the US for increased military aid and a "freer hand in Afghanistan." Rather than kill him or hand him over discreetly, Hersh says the Pakistanis insisted on staging an elaborate American "raid" with Pakistani support. The Navy SEALs met no resistance at Abottabad and were escorted by a Pakistani intelligence officer to bin Laden's bedroom, where they killed him. Bin Laden's body parts were tossed out over the mountains during the flight back not buried at sea. The intelligence materials taken from bin Laden's compound, were manufactured to provide evidence after the fact.

My conclusion that Obama's story is a lie was based on the information given by Obama and his administration. I think that Seymour Hersh has better and wider sources, and his story could be more accurate than mine, but at least **both of us came to the same conclusion that it is a lie**.

9. Comments on the faked story that "Syrian president used poison gases"

I noticed that the claims of the USA that the Syrian regime used chemical weapons against its people on August 2013 were lies. I determined that Kerry was lying from his own statements:
"We know that for three days before the attack the Syrian regime's chemical weapons personnel were on the ground in the area making preparations. And we know that the Syrian regime elements were told to prepare for the attack by putting on gas masks and taking

precautions associated with chemical weapons. We know that these were specific instructions. We know where the rockets were launched from and at what time. We know where they landed and when. We know rockets came only from regime-controlled areas and went only to opposition-controlled or contested neighborhoods." http://www.state.gov/secretary/remarks/2013/08/213668.htm

The lies of these statements are evident from simple analysis. The areas of the chemical attacks were under the control of the repels, but the statements talk about personnel in the area for three days, making preparations. The preparation for the attack is evacuating the areas and its surroundings, **not going there for three days and putting on gas masks**. There is a suggestion that the preparations were mixing the chemicals, which contradict the use of rockets to deliver the chemical agents. Actually, I believed that ISIS is the one behind this attack because they are the only one capable of doing such atrocities, mass beheadings, and mass killing. The statements ignored to answer the real question; **IS Obama honestly interested in protecting the lives of innocent people, or the legitimacy of governments**. What about the hundreds of thousands killed is Iraq and Syria. The kind of legitimacy the USA is promoting is the freedom of powerful countries to kill the innocent people without any punishment and make up stories to justify that. To complete the picture, the **Islamic organizations** called on Obama to attack Syria, as if there is a war between Islam and the Syrian regime, and the USA is the protector of Islam.

Ironically, Seymour Hersh also disclosed that this story is a lie, like the story of the Iraqi's weapons of mass destruction. He concluded that the attack by chemical weapons had been launched by the al-Qaeda franchise Jabhat al-Nusra, and later indicated that Turkey was involved in it.

10. Comments on the "Full Success Of Obama To Support ISIS"

Some people look at ISIS's situation and its growing strength, in spite of Obama's war against them, thinking that it is indication of the complete failure of Obama's policy, I disagree with this assessment. Any reasonable person can recognize that when the most powerful nation and its allies, allow Islamic terrorists to kill innocent people, loot their properties, and enslave their women and children, the guaranteed results will be to enrich, embolden, and strengthen the terrorists. Hence, **Obama's policy was actually to support those Islamic terrorists, not to defeat them, which he now successfully achieved**.

Obama claimed that the USA would train about 2000 moderate Moslems to fight ISIL, and ended with only five trainees and hundreds of millions of dollars spent to arm ISIL instead of fighting them. **This ratio of 4 to 2000 is an accurate representation of the real ratio of what Obama calls Moderate Moslems to other Moslems**. This proves again my points, mentioned before, about the non-existence of moderate Moslems.

Now, with the crisis of migrants from Syria, there are important questions:

1. Are those migrants really from Syria not Turkey or ISIS?
2. Why they want to go specifically to Germany (notice that Germany is the target country for Turkish migrants)?
3. Why no one cared when the non-Moslems were slaughtered?
4. Why these migrants did not go to surrounding countries?
5. Why Obama wants to bring tens of thousands of Moslem migrants to the USA?
6. Why the USA, Western countries, and the International communities did not help them stay to fight ISIS and defend their lives, homes, and country instead of migrating to foreign countries?
7. What about Boko Haram and El-Shabab terrorists?
8. What about the human rights in Saudi Arabia, Sudan, El Bahrain, Iran, etc.?

Notice that Obama is doing his double hit again, like the one when he released five Moslem terrorists and one American spy (Bergdahl) for nothing to support the Islamic terror. Now, he is planning to bring thousands of Moslems that support ISIS from Syria to the USA as refugees??!! Are they Moslems suffering from Islamic discrimination??!! Where was he when Christians were prosecuted and beheaded? Obama's administration stated that they did a through investigation to select those migrants. The**American**

11. Comments on the San Bernardino Massacre

On December 2, 2015, 14 people were killed and 22 were seriously injured in an Islamic terrorist attack in San Bernardino, California. It took Obama four days to say that it was a terrorist attack, without admitting the fact that it was an **Islamic terrorist attack**. This massacre happened few days after Obama said that the USA is safe and encouraged everyone to live his life as usual. From Obama's speech about this massacre [https://www.whitehouse.gov/the-press-office/2015/12/06/address-nation-president], we can see that he lives in denial. I am going to quote him and comment as follow:

1- Obama said; "But it is clear that the two of them had gone down the dark path of radicalization, embracing a perverted interpretation of Islam that calls for war against America and the West". He admits, in a twisted way, the goals of the terrorists, which is not only against the west but also against all non-Moslems. He wrongfully claims that their ideology is **perverted interpretation of Islam**, while it is the **true teachings of Islam** as explained before.

2- Obama said; "Intelligence and law enforcement agencies have disrupted countless plots here and overseas, and worked around the clock to **keep us safe**". No doubt that this massacre is **his** kind of safety he invited people to enjoy. He talked about disrupting plots that no one saw, while hiding the **miserable failure** of these agencies to prevent the Boston, and San Bernardino's massacres (those failures should be criminally investigated).

3- Obama said; "terrorists turned to less complicated acts of violence like the mass shootings that are all **too common** in our society. It is this type of attack that we saw at Fort Hood in 2009; in

151

Chattanooga earlier this year; and now in San Bernardino". He is equating the terror of mad individuals not supported by anyone, to that of an **ideology** that has more than a **billion followers** around the world, and **millions inside the US**, and is **heavily financed** and supported internationally.

4- Obama said; "First, our military will continue to hunt down terrorist plotters in any country where it is necessary". He did not tell us how he did this hunt for El-Shabab and Boko-Haram.

5- Obama said; "Second, we will continue to provide training and equipment to tens of thousands of Iraqi and Syrian forces fighting ISIL - - ". He forgot to tell us that those **thousands he trained joined ISIL except 4 persons**, and all these **equipment went to ISIL**, what a great way to support terrorists??!!!

6- Obama said; "Third, we're working with friends and allies to stop ISIL's operations - -. Since the attacks in Paris, we've surged intelligence-sharing with our European allies. We're working with **Turkey** to seal its border with Syria. And we are cooperating with Muslim-majority countries -- and with our Muslim communities here at home -- to counter the **vicious** ideology that ISIL promotes online. But the fact is that our intelligence and law enforcement agencies -- no matter how effective they are -- cannot identify every **would-be mass shooter**, whether that individual is motivated by ISIL or some other **hateful ideology**". Why he did not share this intelligence before Paris's attack?! Another sad joke is that Obama is working with **Turkey**, which is the largest supporter of ISIL. The irony he is working with Muslim-majority countries like Saudi Arabia and Qatar, and on the same time, every one knows that they are the major source of terrorists' ideology. Obama must be removed from office for not knowing how to identify every **would-be mass shooter**. Can Obama explain to us what he means by some other **hateful ideology,** and if there was any action taken against it.

7- Obama said; "We cannot turn against one another by letting this fight be defined as a war between America and Islam". This fight is actually between the entire world and the terror of Islam. On the same time, we should not accuse every Moslem with terrorism, or ask them to **leave the country, except** when they show us that they **do not believe in our constitution or our standards**.

8- Obama said; "It is our responsibility to reject religious tests on who we admit into this country". As if Obama did not know about the rules giving asylum to religiously prosecuted minorities like Christians in the Middle East. He wants to reverse these rules to allow the Moslem majorities that prosecute Christians to migrate to the USA to spread their terror, and deprive their victims from seeking asylum in the USA, ignoring that this religious test is necessary to know if a person qualifies for asylum due to the prosecution of his religion. Why Obama is bringing Moslems to the USA? Are those Shia-Moslems escaping the discrimination of Sunni Moslems or Christians? If they are, why we do not let them go to a Shia neighboring country like Iran, Iraq, or Elbahrain? Are those Sunni-Moslems escaping the discrimination of Shia Moslems or Christians? If they are, why we do not let them go to a Sunni neighboring country like Turkey, Saudi Arabia, or Qatar? We all understand that the Christians has no place to go in this rejoin, hence, the only places to go is the USA or western countries.

Obviously, Obama is twisting the facts and the rules, to achieve his hidden agenda. Why he did not decry (if it was not American) that; Islamic countries and Muslims (including the non-radical) does not allow building or even repairing churches or Jewish places; does not allow non-Muslims to enter their countries; burn other than Islamic books; does not allow freedom of speech; does not allow freedom of religion; kill any one who preaches other religions; humiliate and discriminate against non-Muslims; kill the non-Muslims and loot their properties; etc. Obama is very well aware about how Muslims brutally kill the non-Moslems and other Muslims that think differently, and he wants to bring them to the USA to spread their brutalities.

Obama ignored the fact that San Bernardino terrorists were not recruited by ISIS, they were **motivated by their deep believes in the true teachings of Islam**. These teachings turned them against the country that sheltered them, gave them good jobs, freedom of speech, freedom of religion, and the opportunity to get every thing a human can get. They not only stabbed their country, but also, brutally killed innocent people that **took them as friends, and did EXACTLY what Islam ordered them** {"O you who believe! Do not take the Jews and the Christians for friends. They are friends one to another. Who, among you who **takes them for friends is (one) of them**. Allah will not guide the wrong doers." [Quran 5:51]}.

What happened in San Bernardino are exactly the teachings of Islam and its Taqyiah principle, that the world knew for centuries, and Barak Housin Obama is USING THIS TAQYIAH NOW TO HIDE THE ISLAMIC FACTS.